EDINBURGH
Past and Present

EDINBURGH

Past and Present

Maurice Lindsay
and
David Bruce

ROBERT HALE · LONDON

ISBN 0 7090 4032 6

Robert Hale Limited
Clerkenwell House
Clerkenwell Green
London EC1R 0HT

Set in Ehrhardt by
Derek Doyle & Associates, Mold, Clwyd
Printed in Great Britain by
St Edmundsbury Press, Bury St Edmunds, Suffolk
Bound by WBC Bookbinders

Contents

Acknowledgements

The sources of the Victorian photographs are as follows:

Edinburgh City Libraries: 1(a), 2(a), 4(a), 24(a), 38(a), 39(a).

Scottish Photography Archive: 1(b), 3(a), 5(a), 6(a), 7(a), 8(a), 9(a), 10(a), 11(a), 12(a), 15(a), 16(a), 17(a), 18(a), 19(a), 20(a), 21(a), 25(a), 26(a), 27(a), 28(a) – (c), 29(a), 30(a), 32(a), 33(a), 35(a), 36(a), 40(a), 41(a), 42(a), 43(a), 44(a).

Royal Scottish Academy: 13(a), 14(a).

Royal Commission on the Ancient and Historical Monuments of Scotland – National Monuments Record: 22(a), 23(a), 31(a), 34(a), 37(a).

Glasgow University Library: 45(a), 45(c), 45(e), 45(g).

The authors acknowledge with gratitude the contribution of the Scottish Photography Archive to this volume. In particular, we are indebted for access to the recently acquired Riddell Collection from which several images are drawn. We thank Miss Sara Stevenson and Mrs Julie Lawson for all their assistance in our work with the SPA. We must also thank Miss Norma Armstrong of Edinburgh District Libraries for her ready help in answering our queries. Thanks are due, too, to Mrs Doris Cairns and Mrs Kathleen Smith for typing assistance.

The authors wish to thank the following for permission to reproduce copyright material: Robert Garrioch, Norman MacCaig, Moray MacLaren and Helga Young. They would also like to thank John Calder Ltd for permission to quote Sidney Goodsir–Smith's poem 'Under the Eildon Tree' from his *Collected Poems* (John Calder), and David Higham Associates for a poem by Ruthven Todd from *Garland for a Winter Solstice* (Weidenfeld).

All the modern photographs are the work of the late Murray Johnston (1949–90). It is a matter of great sadness that Murray died, after a long illness, before this book was completed. He was born in Dundee and studied photography in Edinburgh before beginning a varied photographic career which included studio administration, being the first photographer in residence in Keilder Forest,

Northumberland, and becoming Director of Stills Gallery in Edinburgh. He lectured at Edinburgh College of Art and supported contemporary Scottish photography by means of the company, Scottish Photographic Works, which he set up with his wife Kate. His own photographs have been shown in a number of one-man and group exhibitions throughout Britain and the USA and he is represented in several private and public collections.

New Edinburgh, Auld Reekie

The Fabric of History

1

The City in History

It is surprising for how short a time it has been possible to preserve an accurate visual record of human life and living-conditions. We imagine what dinosaurs and their kind looked like from skeletal reconstructions, but our knowledge of the appearance of early man is largely conjectural, if probably fairly accurate.

True, in cave sites, such as Les Eyzies, in France, primitive art, showing hunting scenes and domestic animals, has survived, painfully scratched on the rough walls. Medieval life was illustrated, so to say, in the flat. It was not until the discovery of perspective that artists could produce anything like an accurate representation of what happened before their eyes. The invention of photography, which for all practical purposes reached Scotland in the 1840s, introduced a new element of visual precision.

Long before attempts to represent life in Edinburgh by visual or pictorial means were successful, writers had been recording what went on round about them. We therefore have a fairly comprehensive account of what Edinburgh life was like in the days before the camera set about freezing into stillness a few of the countless millions of Edinburgh's passing images.

While a major feature of this book is its illustrations of the physical changes which have affected the city since the first cameras recorded what the place looked like to early and mid-Victorian citizens, the purpose of this chapter is not only to set the historical background in which the early photographers sought their subject-matter but also to record through the eyes of the poets and writers of prose how the Edinburgh way of life seemed to them before the camera was invented.

Today, in the last decade of the twentieth century, Edinburgh is a capital city which houses the Scottish part of the British governmental apparatus under a Secretary of State for Scotland whose first duty is, inevitably, to implement British policy as it affects Scotland. There are those who think that arrangement affects Scotland's status as a nation. To put it mildly, it is doubtful if the slightly dotty image created by the Scottish National Party, which came into being in the 1920s, is ever likely to cause more than an occasional diversional fizz, like an exploding firework by the wayside of an organized central display. Scottish Nationalism's original appeal was, and remains, mainly a romantic one; yet, as the Aberdeen poet G.S. Fraser put it:

With Byron and with Lermontov
  Romantic Scotland's in the grave.

The Devolutionists, on the other hand, take rather more cognizance of 'the limitations of necessity', the late twentieth century's day-to-day practical realities. Since newspaper polls regularly suggest that a clear majority of Scots want some form of devoluted government for all except shared British concerns, and since the Labour Party has adopted as official policy the intention of creating such a thing when next it is in power, it seems likely that Scottish Devolution will sooner or later become a reality – for all I know, perhaps sooner than the interval of time between my writing this and my words appearing in print.

Today Edinburgh enjoys a thriving tourist trade, vying with Stratford-upon-Avon as Britain's second most popular attraction, after London. It promotes – some might nowadays say tolerates – a three-week-long International Festival of Music and Drama in the late summer; an event which has survived through most of the latter half of the century. Founded in 1947, it was at first one of the world's greatest international cultural celebrations, a rare salute to some of the finest achievements of the human spirit in the Western world. Latterly, however, partly through chronic and sustained official under-funding and recently a mistaken populist effort to broaden its appeal, it has, paradoxically, forfeited much of its world standing; indeed, it no longer appears quite certain what it should really be about, or where it should be going.

Culturally, Glasgow, home of the Scottish National Orchestra, Scottish Opera, Scottish Ballet, the Burrell Collection, the Citizen's Theatre and a splendid new concert hall commemorating 1990, its year as European City of Culture, has long since overtaken Edinburgh. Since Edinburgh has dismally failed over decades to face up to its traffic problems – again, unlike Glasgow, whose Inner Ring Road lost it only one B-listed building – the commuter approaching or leaving the city during the morning or evening rush-hours finds himself incarcerated in a slow-moving traffic-jam not dissimilar to those which contribute so markedly to the decline in the quality of life in London itself.

Edinburgh's greatest assets are its castle, reared on a rock in the centre of the city; its Old and New Towns, rescued and restored in the nick of time; and the quality of its light. On a clear, windy day – and Edinburgh has many of them – the light seems almost to take wings, illuminating a detail here, winning attention for a hitherto unnoticed elevation there. With so much of its population traditionally involved in the running of Church and State, and its latter-day effective concern with banking and insurance, there is a quality of douceness about its people, a quiet, conservative reaction which perhaps encourages the rigorous initiatives of its imported official galleries directors and the showbizzing opportunism of some of its native impresarios.

In the end, though, it is the fabric of the city that wins the hearts of its visitors, drawn, perhaps, in the first place, by the stories and dark, half-legendary remnants of Scottish history once played out within its bounds; stories and legends which provided one of its greatest sons, Sir Walter Scott, with the material facts that his imagination immortalized in the Waverley Novels.

Few of the greatest writers from Scotland's past were unfamiliar with Auld Reekie, as Edinburgh used to be called when smoke from its piled-up hilly chimneys curled off the spine of its Old Town, like steam from a drying animal. William Dunbar, one of Scotland's three finest poets, served James IV. Robert Burns, the greatest of the three, spent two winters at first charming, and then to some extent alarming, its polite society. Hugh MacDiarmid, the third of the great poets, frequently held garrulous court in one or other of its Rose Street pubs. James Boswell brought Samuel Johnson to the Edinburgh of that short-lived laureate of town life Robert Fergusson. Robert Louis Stevenson, born and bred in its professional circle, carried away images of the city in his heart during his final years as a South Sea exile.

I shall, in due course, call upon almost all of them, along with some of their latter-day successors, to illustrate my outline of the Edinburgh story which, during the last century and a half the camera has counterpointed. But, first of all, some facts.

The Sloping Mile

Although Edinburgh did not become the official capital of Scotland until the middle of the fifteenth century, the cliff of basalt rock – an extinct volcano – round which the city grew probably carried defensive fortifications of some sort in the days of the Picts and the Romans. An early castle was occupied by Malcolm Canmore, the first king of a more or less united Scotland, in the eleventh century. That castle may still have been built partly of wood, like its predecessors, but it was lived in by Alexander I and declared a royal domain by David I, from whose reign the oldest surviving building, St Margaret's Chapel, probably dates. The stump of David II's tower house on the rock is now embedded in the Half Moon Battery of 1573. The castle which dominates the late twentieth-century skyline dates mostly from the sixteenth and seventeenth centuries, with later alterations and additions.

At the lower end of the sloping mile, which relaxes its rugged spine downhill from the castle, lies the palace of Holyroodhouse begun by David I. Only the ruined chapel is Norman. Of the palace itself, James IV's L-plan tower house was unfinished when he was killed at Flodden in 1514. James V made notable additions. Much was destroyed during Hertford's 'rough wooing' of 1544–5, when he sought the hand of the infant Mary, Queen of Scots, for the son of his English sovereign, Henry VIII. As it now presents itself to us, the symmetry of Holyroodhouse is largely the work of a seventeenth-century architect, Sir William Bruce.

Between these two controlling royal extremities, the shape of much of Scotland's history was formed. Although the early Stuart kings reputedly preferred their castle of Stirling, James V made frequent use of Edinburgh Castle. His daughter, the future Mary, Queen of Scots, however, was born in Linlithgow Palace; but Mary in her turn bore the future James VI within the walls of Edinburgh Castle. After James VI rode south to inherit English Elizabeth's throne in 1603, Holyrood was used only occasionally as a royal residence; as, indeed, it still is today. It capitulated to the forces of Prince Charles Edward Stuart during his southward march in 1745. Within its walls he held a glittering Jacobite levee, though the castle up the hill just managed to hold firm for the government.

Between these royal residences, too, the ordinary homes of the inhabitants of the Old Town of Edinburgh were tightly packed, dwellings crowding both flanks of the 'spine', stretching at right angles to the High Street. Within this concentrated area, defended by the city walls, popular reaction to the struggles of the Reformation, the strident religious disputations of the seventeenth century and the loss of the Scottish Parliament in 1707, was vigorously enacted. From these cramped homes, too, came the men responsible for the intellectual flowering of the eighteenth century, the 'Athens of the North' phase of Edinburgh's story. With the reins of government removed from Scottish hands and tightening increasingly, Scotland turned to learning and the arts in a remarkable intellectual upsurge by European standards, culminating in the philosophy of David Hume, the political economy of Adam Smith, the journalistic and autobiographical work of James Boswell (thanks to whose persistence Dr Johnson was lured to Scotland in 1773), the Scots verse of Allan Ramsay and, as already mentioned, Robert Fergusson, the laureate of Edinburgh who died in a madhouse tragically young. Into these streets rode Robert Burns during the winter months of 1786–7, to carry on his love-affair with 'Clarinda', the widow Agnes Maclehose, and for a time to experience the heady sensation of being romantically lionized as the supposedly 'heaven-taught ploughman'.

Moving amongst such men, whose names are nowadays on every educated tongue, were others only a little less distinguished in the fields of medicine, the law, university administration and the Church. It was the Edinburgh which, a little later, produced the diarist and judge Lord Cockburn and, of course, nourished the great mind of Sir Walter Scott, whose narrative poems and Waverley Novels awoke Scotland to the sense of her historic past as, a generation before, Burns's poems had awakened her to the subtle social and musical overtones of her Lowland Scots language. Scott's work in particular carried an image of Scotland to Europe, helping to fire the Romantic imagination. From the presses of the Old Town, too, came William Smellie's *Encyclopaedia Britannica* in 1771, and the first of that clutch of battling literary magazines, eagerly read periodicals such as the original *Edinburgh Review*, to be followed by the *Quarterly Review* and *Blackwoods*, to say nothing of *The Scotsman* newspaper, founded in 1817. *The Scotsman* was edited in the Old Town, as it still is, but *Blackwoods* moved across to George Street. Though they were unquestionably influential, the circulation of these magazines by modern standards was not great. There was probably a maximum serious readership of about 2,000 people in the Scotland of the 1820s and thirties – some would say that modern readership for literary magazines and books is no greater. The magazines were, however, avidly studied by what would nowadays be called 'the opinion-formers', not only in Scotland but also in England and in the New World of America.

Poets and Pipers

Numerous accounts and vignettes of Old Town life have come down to us, some written by poets, others in the form of prose, as diary or journal comment.

The Edinburgh of James IV, which the poet William Dunbar knew, with its high houses squeezed tightly within the defendable city, suffered greatly from fires, the worst of which took place in 1532, the year in which the High Street was first paved, an innovation much commented upon by visitors. Indeed, because of the fire danger, an order had to be made prohibiting the storing of heather and peat before doors.

If he escaped death in a 'high-rise' land or tenement fire, a citizen of Dunbar's time might well succumb to bubonic plague, which, when it broke out, leapt as agilely as fire across the narrow wynds (side streets). Even if he survived both these hazards, there were other offences against both eyes and nostrils which had to be put up with:

Why will ye, merchants of renoun,
Lat Edinburgh, your nobil toun,
For lack of reformatioun
The common profit tine, and game?   [lose
    Think ye not shame,
That ony other regioun
Sall, with dishonour hurt your name!

May nane pass through your princeful gaits   [ways
For stink of haddocks and of skates,
For crys of carlings and debates,   [common people
For fensum flytings of defame: [loud scoldings
    Think ye not shame,
Before strangers of all estatis
That sic dishonour hurt your name!

Your stinkand Schule, that standis dirk   [dark
Halds the licht fra your parroch kirk;   [St Giles
Your foirstairs maks your housis mirk,
Like na country bot here at hame:
    Think ye not shame,
Sa little policy to wirk
In hurt and sclander of your name!

At your hie Cross, whar gold and silk
Suld be, there is bot curds and milk;
And at your Tron bot cockle and wilk,
Pansches, puddings of Jock and Jame: [tripe
    Think ye not shame,
Sen as the warld sayis that ilk,
In hurt and sclander of your name! ...

The fire of 1532, however, induced improvements, which led an anonymous English traveller of the 1530s to become quite eloquent in Edinburgh's praise: 'There are two spacious streets,' he recorded, 'of which the principal one, leading from the Palace to the Castle, is paved with square stones. The City itself is not built of bricks, but of square freestones, and so stately is its appearance that single houses may be compared to palaces. From the Abbey to the Castle there is a continued street, which on both sides contains a range of excellent houses.'

This favourable impression is confirmed by later sixteenth-century travellers. The scholar Fynes Moryson, for instance, observed in 1591 a city 'high seated, in a fruitful soil, and wholesome air ... adorned with many Noblemen's Towers lying about it' and abounding in 'many springs and sweet waters'. Moryson commented on the 'park of hares, conies [rabbits] and deer in a high mountain ... called the chair of Arthur'. He also praised 'the broad and very fair street', the High Street, though he felt that the individual houses would have made a 'fair show ... but that the outside of them' were 'faced with wooden galleries, built upon the second story of the house'. He admitted, though, that these galleries gave the inhabitants 'a fair and pleasant prospect into the said fair, and broad street'.

Sir William Brereton, a Yorkshire soldier with a notebook, travelling to broaden his mind (he later became a Member of Parliament and a commander with the anti-Royalist forces during the Civil War), arrived in Edinburgh late in June 1634. He, too, thought the city situated in 'a dainty, healthful pure air'. The inhabitants, however, he found nasty and slothful: 'The Slutishness and nastiness of this people,' he protested, 'is such that I cannot omit the particularizing thereof.... Their houses and halls and kitchens have such a noisesome taste, a savour, and that so strong, as it doth offend you so soon as you come within their walls. Yea, sometimes when I have light from my horse, I felt the distaste of it before I have come into the house.... I never went to my own lodging in Edinburgh, or went out, but I am constrained to hold my nose, or to use wormwood, or some such scented plant.'

'Slutishness' was a constant complaint against Scots inns and their staffs well into the eighteenth century. The accountant Edward Burt, who accompanied the road-building, Highlander-pacifying General Wade into Scotland in 1724 (Wade had been military land commander during the rising of 1715), when entering a High Street inn found much to distress him:

The cook was too filthy an object to be described; only another English gentleman whispered to me and said, he believed, if the fellow was to be thrown against the wall, he would stick to it.

Twisting round and round his hand a greasy towel, he stood waiting to know what we would have for supper, and mentioned several things himself; among the rest, a duke, a fool, or a mere-fool. This was nearly according to his pronunciation; but he meant a duck, a fowl, or a moor-fowl, or grouse.

We supped very plentifully, and drank good French claret, and were very merry till the clock struck ten, the hour when everybody is at liberty, by beat of the city drum, to throw their filth out at the windows. Then the company began to light pieces of paper and throw them upon the table to smoke the room and, as I thought, to mix one bad smell with another.

Being in my retreat to pass through a long narrow wynde or alley, to go to my new lodgings, a guide was assigned me, who went before me to prevent my disgrace, crying out all the way, with a loud voice, 'Hud your haunde'. The throwing of a sash, or otherwise opening a window, made me tremble, while behind and before me, at some little distance, fell the terrible shower.

Well, I escaped all the danger and arrived, not only safe and sound, but sweet and clean, at my new quarters; but when I was in bed I was forced to hide my head between the sheets; for the smell of the filth, thrown out by the neighbours on the back side of the house, came pouring into the room to such a degree, I was almost poisoned by the stench.

Such an experience confronted alike ordinary travellers and the famous. Among the most distinguished of travellers was the great lexicographer Dr Samuel Johnson. Filled with disbelief in the genuineness of the supposed Gaelic originals of James Macpherson's Ossianic epic poems, Dr Johnson allowed himself to be persuaded by Boswell to come north and seek out proof or disproof himself.

Johnson set out from London on his tour to the Western Isles of Scotland on Friday 6 August 1773. He travelled to Newcastle in the company of Robert Chambers, the principal of New Inn Hall, Oxford, who was on his way to India to take up the appointment of judge. Together they jogged along in a chaise drawn by a pair of horses, a fairly luxurious means of travel. At Newcastle Chambers' place in the conveyance was taken by William Scott, later to become Lord Stowell, a judge of the High Court of Admiralty. The travellers entered Scotland at Berwick-upon-Tweed and, passing through Haddington, arrived in Edinburgh by the road alongside Holyrood-house, then the main southern approach to the Canongate, at whose foot stood the White Horse Inn, built in 1683 (now restored and converted into flats). The landlord was one James Boyd, who by the time he retired had amassed a fortune of several thousand pounds. Nevertheless, the inn, like virtually all Scottish hostelries of the period, was dirty and wretched; 'crowded and confused' was how a somewhat more charitable anonymous contemporary traveller described it.

Fortunately Johnson had to endure it for only one night, because as soon as Boswell knew his friend had arrived, he rescued Johnson and took him to his own house (as a flat in a land, or tenement, was then called) on the north side of the Lawnmarket, in James's Court. Johnson told Mrs Theale in a letter that his host had 'very handsome and spacious rooms; level on the ground on one side of the house, and on the other four stories high'. Unfortunately the side of the court containing Boswell's home was destroyed by fire in the middle of the nineteenth century. On both the outward visit and during his stay on the return trip south, Johnson was called upon by many of the most eminent citizens of the town. But on Monday 16 August he set out in the company of the historian William Robertson to see 'some of the things which they had to show'. They inspected the exterior of the long-since-removed Weigh House, the Luckenbooths (also long since demolished), the Tollbooth (a grim Gothic building long gone but once the scene of the Porteous Riots, featured in Scott's greatest novel, *The Heart of Midlothian*), Parliament House and the Advocate's Library. In the Laigh (lower) Hall, which then housed the records of Scotland, Johnson, 'rolling about in this old magazine of antiquities', uttered that sentiment which has acted ever since as a spur to authors indolently awaiting some manifestation of genius: 'A man may write at any time if he will set himself doggedly to it.'

At St Giles, he vigorously hoped that John Knox, the Reformer, had been buried in 'a way of common trade', and inspected the cathedral 'that had once been a church'. At that time it was divided into four, in one of which, the New or High Church, Burns's patron Dr Hugh Blair regularly delivered his once-popular but vapidly rhetorical sermons, subsequently issued in handsome leather-bound volumes. From there, Dr Johnson went down a long-since-vanished flight of steps to the Cowgate and up a steep hill to the College, of which Robertson was the principal. At that time the College buildings were mean-looking (the foundation stone of the New College was not laid until 1789), yet it had a high reputation, particularly for its medical faculty, and had between six and seven hundred students.

From the College, Johnson, a man of sixty-three, moved on to inspect the Royal Infirmary, where at that time an inmate's failure to attend divine service resulted in the loss of a meal. Finally Johnson inspected Holyrood Abbey, while Robertson 'fluently harangued' him on scenes from Scottish history.

On the return journey, in November, Johnson and Boswell left Auchinleck (Boswell's family seat, then the home of his father, Lord Auchinleck, the judge) on the 8th, arriving back late the same evening. This time the castle was visited, in between the holding of many levees and the attending of dinner and supper parties. All in all, as he later wrote to his friend the Revd Dr Taylor, vicar of Ashbourne, Derbyshire, Johnson had '... traversed the east coast of Scotland from south to north, from Edinburgh to Inverness, and the west coast from north to south, from the Highlands to Glasgow'. The time he had spent on his tour, he often repeated, was 'the pleasantest part of his life'.

The same year in which Johnson was introduced to Edinburgh, Robert Fergusson published 'Auld Reekie: A Poem', in which he evoked the daily sights and sounds of his native city. There are the servants, who every night unhygienically disposed of the offensive contents of their employers' slop-pails.

> On stair wi' tub, or pot in hand,
> The barefoot housemaids looe to stand, [love
> That antrim fock may ken how snell [casual; sharp
> Auld Reekie will at morning smell:
> Then, with an inundation big as
> The burn that 'neath the Nore Loch brig is,
> They kindly shower Edina's roses
> To quicken and regale our noses.

(The Nor' Loch lay in the hollow between the Old and New Towns of Edinburgh. The bridge over it was put up in 1763.)

'Gardyloo' – from the French *'Gardez l'eau'* – was the cry from above before the contents of pails were decanted into the street from a height of several storeys. This insanitary measure took some eradicating, for even after Edinburgh Town Council had declared such a method of disposing of household slops illegal, half a century later Johnson was still able to observe that at ten o'clock many a splendid head-dress was 'moistened into flaccidity'.

Other evils were practised equally openly. Prostitution, then as now, was a degrading if inevitable trade.

> Near some lamp-post, wi dowy face, [sad
> Wi' heavy een and sour grimace,
> Stands she that beauty lang had kend [known
> Whoredom her trade, and vice her end.
> But see wharenow she wuns her bread [wins
> By that which Nature ne'er decreed;
> And sings sad music to the lugs, [ears
> 'Mang burochs o' damn'd whore and rogues.

A traveller who visited Edinburgh three years after the publication of the original version of Fergusson's poem provided tourists with a new satisfaction-concept, that of the picturesque, a cult-term invented by a Cumbrian-born artist, William Gilpin.

Gilpin, an Oxford graduate and for some years headmaster of Cheam school, came to Scotland with his notebook to gather material for his book, *Observations on several parts of Great Britain, particularly the Highlands of Scotland, relative to Picturesque Beauty, made in the year 1776.* The book did not, however, appear until 1779. Gilpin defined 'picturesque ideas' as lying 'not in the common road of genius and learning'. He thought that they required 'perhaps a distinct faculty to comprehend them ... more attention to the scenes of nature, and the rules of art, than men of letters in general, unless stimulated by a peculiar inclination, bestow upon them'. In other words, Gilpin looked with the eye of a painter, ignoring the immediate emotional relationship between Man and Nature which was later to become the particular concern of Wordsworth.

Gilpin reached Edinburgh high in expectation, having read that the Scottish capital was 'one of the most picturesque towns in Britain'. People, he explained, '... often consider *romantic* and *picturesque* as synonymous'. This was not, in his view, so. He instanced Arthur's Seat: 'Arthur's Seat, which is still the principal object, appears still as odd, mishapen, and uncouth.... It gave us the idea of a cap of maintenance in heraldry; and a view with such a strong feature in it can no more be picturesque than a face with a bulbous nose can be beautiful.' However, '... the town and castle, indeed, on the left, made some amends....' When he came to leave Edinburgh for Stirling, Arthur's Seat again made him shudder and declare: 'Arthur's Seat presents an unpleasing view from every station.'

Edinburgh as a whole, however, stood up to the test of being examined by Gilpin from all sides: 'As you approach from the south, it appears like a grand city of noble extent. As you move to the right, its size gradually diminishes. But when you view it from the Musselborough road, which is in a direction due east, the street is gone; and the houses are all crowded together, as if they had retreated under the walls of the castle. And yet the appearance of the town and castle, thus united by perspective into one vast object, is extremely grand.'

Indeed, he thought that 'the only object of picturesque curiosity in Edinburgh' was the castle. 'Those who go to see it are commonly satisfied with being carried *into* it,' he noted, 'where they find a number of patched, incoherent buildings without any beauty.... But he who would see Edinburgh Castle in perfection must go to the bottom of the rock it stands on and walk round it. The rock, which is in itself an amazing pile, is in many parts nobly broken; and tho', in its whole immensity, it is too large an object for a picture, unless at a proper distance, yet many of its craggy corners, with their watch-towers and other appendages, are very picturesque.'

Holyroodhouse was dismissed as being simply 'a grand palace, occupying a large square'.

A year after Dr Johnson dubbed the empty diambeo slops 'the flowers of Edinburgh' ('Sir, I can smell you in the dark,' the great man quipped to Boswell on one occasion), Edward Topham, the 24-year-old son of a York lawyer, was sent to Edinburgh at the conclusion of the European Grand Tour, to be 'finished'. He kept an entertaining diary of his experiences.

Topham arrived at an inn in the Pleasance (a part of the Old Town that had become a slum by the end of the nineteenth century and has been entirely rebuilt in the twentieth) to be greeted by a 'poor devil of a girl without shoes or stockings, and with only a single linsey-woolsey petticoat, which just reached half-way to her ankles', who showed him into a room in which about twenty Scots drovers were drinking whisky and eating potatoes. Topham was then offered a share of a bed with a newly arrived stage-coach traveller. This he declined, moving up to the home of 'a good dame by the Cross' in the High Street, who kept a coffee-house, where he was given an apartment in a land 'six stories high'.

One of the most widely read English travellers of the period, Thomas Pennant (1726–98), the son of an ancient Flintshire family, had a keen interest in scientific matters. When elected to the Royal Society of Uppsala, he met the Swedish naturalist Linnaeus. Later, on a visit to France, Pennant encountered Voltaire – 'very entertaining and a master of English oaths'. On 26 June 1769, 'struck … with the reflection of having never seen Scotland', Pennant set out from his home in Chester, travelling by way of Macclesfield, Lincoln, Hull, Scarborough, Durham, Newcastle, Alnwick, Berwick and so across the border. After crossing the Esk at Musselburgh, he reached Edinburgh on 18 July.

The impression the Edinburgh skyline made upon him as he approached the city was of boldness and grandeur: 'The view of the houses at a distance strikes the traveller with wonder; their loftiness, improved by their almost aerial situation, gives them a look of magnificence not to be found in any other part of Great Britain. All these conspicuous buildings form the upper part of the great street, are made of stone, and make a handsome appearance: they are generally six or seven stories high in front, but by reason of the declivity of the hill, much higher backward.... Every house has a common staircase, and every story is the habitation of a separate family.'

As a Chester man, Pennant was, of course, aware of the limitations of a walled city: 'It must be observed, that this unfortunate species of architecture arose from the turbulence of the times in which it was in vogue: everybody was desirous of getting as near as possible to the protection of the castle; the houses crowded together, and I may say, piled one upon another, merely on the principle of security.'

Pennant visited the Advocate's Library and was much impressed by the range of books he saw there. He also inspected St Giles Cathedral (then still divided internally into four churches), Holyroodhouse, Heriot's ('a fine old building, much too magnificent for the end proposed, that of educating poor children'), the College ('a mean building') and the Royal Infirmary ('a spacious and handsome edifice, capable of containing two hundred patients' and with 'an operation room particularly convenient').

From further afield than Chester came one of the most distinguished Europeans to visit Edinburgh in the late eighteenth century, B. Faujas St-Fond (1741–1819), who held several official appointments in France, finishing up as Professor of Geology at the Musée d'Histoire Naturelle in Paris. He much admired the English scientist Sir Joseph Banks who, when President of the Royal Society, had written an account of the basaltic island of Staffa, off Mull, in the Hebrides, which inspired St-Fond with a desire to see it for himself. To achieve this end, he came to Scotland in 1784. His mission successfully accomplished, he arrived in Edinburgh in the company of one Count Andreoni and was introduced to the university circle – in particular to William Cullen, Professor of the Practice of Medicine; James Gregory, Professor of the Institute of Medicine (and the inventor of a laxative, 'Gregory Powder', still horribly and acutely in use when I was a child); Joseph Black, one of the fathers of modern chemistry; Joseph Hutton, then busily engaged in writing what was to become a classic of geology, his *Theory of the Earth, or an Investigation of the Laws observable in the composition, dissolution and restoration of land upon the globe*; and, undoubtedly the greatest of all these eminent men, Adam Smith, author of *The Wealth of Nations*. They talked of Voltaire and Rousseau, whom Smith had met when he lived in Paris. They also talked about Highland music.

One day, at nine o'clock in the morning, Smith came to St-Fond's lodgings and took him off to 'a spacious concert room' full of people, landlords from the Highlands and Islands, Smith explained, come to judge a piping competition. St-Fond's description of the ensuing proceedings is quite in his best manner:

A few moments later, a folding door opened at the bottom of the room, and to my great surprise, I saw a Scottish Highlander enter ... playing upon the bagpipe, and walking up and down the empty space with rapid steps and a military air, blowing the noisiest and most discordant sounds from an instrument which lacerates the ear. The air he played was a kind of sonata, divided into three parts. Smith begged me to give it my whole attention, and to tell him afterwards the impression it made on me.

But I confess that at first I could distinguish neither air nor design. I only saw the piper marching always with rapidity, and with the same warlike countenance. He made incredible efforts both with his body and his fingers to bring into play at once the different pipes of his instrument, which made an insupportable uproar.

He received nevertheless great applause from all sides. A second musician followed into the arena, wearing the same martial look and walking to and fro with the same haughty air.... After having listened to eight pipers in succession, I began to suspect that the first part was connected with a warlike march and military evolutions: the second with a sanguinary battle, which the musician sought to depict by the noise and rapidity of his playing and by his loud cries. He seemed then to be convulsed; his pantomimical gestures resembled those of a man engaged in combat; his arms, his hands, his head, his legs, were all in motion; the sounds of his instrument were all called forth and confounded together at the same moment. This fine disorder seemed keenly to interest every one. The piper then passed, without transition, to a kind of andante; his convulsions suddenly ceased; the sounds of his instrument were plaintive, languishing, as if lamenting the slain who were being carried off from the eyes of the beautiful Scottish ladies. But the whole was so uncouth and extraordinary; the impression which this wild music made upon the inhabitants of the country is such that I am convinced we should look upon this strange composition not as essentially belonging to music, but to history ....

The same air was played by each competitor, of whom there was a considerable number. The most perfect equality was maintained among them; the son of the laird stood on the same footing with the simple shepherd, often belonging to the same clan, bearing the same name, and having the same garb. No preference was shown here save to talent, as I could judge from the hearty plaudits given to some who seemed to excel in that art. I confess that it was impossible for me to admire any of them. I thought them all of equal proficiency; that is to say, the one was as bad as the other; and the air that was played, as well as the instrument itself, involuntarily put me in mind of a bear's dance.

Faujas St-Fond, thus subjected to a native competition, had little of a general nature to say about Edinburgh. Although he stayed in what was probably Edinburgh's first reasonably good hotel, Dunn's, in the New Town, he complained that they charged 'threepence for half a sheet of notepaper and sixpence for the trouble of fetching it' and that by London standards all its charges seemed exorbitant.

Late eighteenth-century Edinburgh abounded in club life. Robert

Chalmers, the antiquarian, tells us, for example, of one of Edinburgh's numerous clubs that was associated with the Lawnmarket or upper part of the High Street.

The Lawnmarket Club was composed mainly of the woollen traders of that street, a set of whom met every morning at about seven o'clock and walked down to the Post Office where they made themselves acquainted with the news of the morning. After a plentiful discussion of the news, they adjourned to a public house, and got a dram of brandy.... They were always the first persons in the town to have a thorough knowledge of the foreign news; and on Wednesday mornings, when there was no post from London, it was their wont to meet, as usual, and amuse themselves by the invention of what was imaginary; and this they made it their business to circulate among the uninitiated acquaintances in the course of the forenoon. Any such unfounded articles of intelligence ... were usually called Lawnmarket Gazettes in allusion to their ... originators.

Lord Cockburn, in his *Memorials of his Time*, recalled another High Street scene from his childhood, the lean-to shopping centre known as The Krames:

It was a long narrow arcade of booths crammed in between the north side of St Giles' Cathedral and a thin range of buildings that stood parallel to the Cathedral, the eastmost of which, looking down the High Street, was the famous shop of William Creech, the bookseller. Shopless traffickers first began to nestle there about the year 1550 to 1560 and their successors stuck to the spot until 1817.... In my boyhood their little stands, each enclosed in a tiny room of its own, and during the day all open to the little foot-path that ran between the two rows of them, and all glittering with attractions, contained everything fascinating to childhood, but chiefly toys. It was like one of the Arabian Nights' bazaars in Baghdad. Throughout the whole year it was enchantment.

The gradual overtaking in social status of the Old Town by the New led also to changes in the style of home entertaining. Little of this had been possible in the Old Town, where men and women alike repaired to the taverns – dingy, candle-lit cellars where they could enjoy oysters:

A crum o' tripe, ham, dish o' pease   [small helping
An egg, or cauler frae the seas,   [herring
   A flook or fightin',
A nice beef steak; or ye may get
A guid buffed herring, reisted skate
An' ingans, an' (though past its date)
   A cut o' veal.

Once the ladies had finished such a repast and had been escorted back to the turnpike stairs of their homes, the men retreated to the taverns for the serious business of drinking, an activity officially meant to end at the sound of the ten o'clock drum but often carried on long after, those who set out unsteadily homewards to the sound of the drum having to keep a wary ear open for the dreaded cry of 'Gardyloo'.

Such things were managed very much more discreetly in the New Town. There, too, other fashions changed as society enlarged itself. Mrs Andrew Fletcher, a Yorkshire woman who married a Scottish Whig solicitor and lived much of her life in Edinburgh, recorded her impressions of the New Town eating-habits of 1811: 'Large dinner-parties were less frequent, and supper parties – I mean hot suppers – were generally discarded. In their place came large evening parties (sometimes larger than the rooms could conveniently hold) where card-playing generally gave place to music or conversation. Many met at nine, and parted at twelve o'clock. Tea and coffee were handed about at nine and guests sat down to some light cold refreshment later in the evening. People did not in these parties meet to eat, but talk and listen.' Doubtless the talk was worth listening to. By 1832, however, the year of Scott's death and of the passing of the Reform Bill, the era of Edinburgh's European intellectual supremacy had come to an end.

There have been some who have doubted the depth of root and the genuineness of Edinburgh's 'Athens of the North' phase. In the abandoned church monument to the Napoleonic Wars on Calton Hill, Douglas Young, writing in the middle of the twentieth century, thought Playfair's unfinished pillars on the top of it prophetic:

These chill pillars of fluted stone
shine back the lustre of the leaden sky,
stiff columns clustered on a dolerite hill
in solemn order, an unperfected vision
dimly gleaming. Not at random thrown
like old Greek temples that abandoned lie
with earthquake-riven drums. Rigid and chill
this still-born ruin stands for our derision.

A fine fantasy of the Whig literati
to build a modern Athens in our frore islands,
those elegant oligarchs of the Regency period,
Philhellenic nabobs and the Scots nobility.
As soon expect to meet a bearded Gujerati
stravaiging in a kilt through the uttermost Highlands
or in Princes Street gardens a coy and blushing Nereid.
Athens proved incapable of such mobility.

The historian G.S. Pryde has observed, less cynically: 'No society seems able to live at this level for an unlimited span. Perhaps inevitably, the magical energy spent itself, and from 1830 onwards, though Scotland produced many men and women of distinction, the former brilliance and zest became diluted.'

Lord Cockburn blamed the decline on the reopening of Europe after the Napoleonic Wars and on the appearance of 'a new race of peace-formed youths' who '... came on the stage but with little literature but with a comfortless intensity of political zeal'. While Edinburgh still had much to offer that was to prove of value in British life, in Cockburn's telling phrase, 'the exact old thing was not'.

'East Windy, West Endy'

A new thing was, however, shortly to emerge, for the decline of the Enlightenment made way for activity of a different sort. The first stirrings of social conscience could be seen operating in both Glasgow and Edinburgh. Friendly Societies, giving workers minimal social security and the guarantee of a decent burial, came into being early in the new century. The first mutual company to be founded in Edinburgh, the Scottish Widows' Fund & Life Assurance Society, was set up in 1815, the year of Waterloo. It was followed in 1823 by the Edinburgh Life Assurance Company, which had associations with Sir Walter Scott, and in 1831 by the Scottish Equitable. The Scottish Provident Institution arrived on the scene in 1837. Thus, while Edinburgh might have lost its brief claim to being the intellectual capital of Europe, already it was well on its way to becoming one of the most dependable financial centres of the by now firmly established United Kingdom.

Nowadays it is generally accepted that environment influences the character. Gentlefolk, noblemen, tradesmen, shopkeepers and fiddlers had all shared different flats off the narrow turnpike stairs which wound their way up the Old Town's medieval 'lands'. As the better-off moved over to the more spacious New Town's 'draughty parallelograms' (as Robert Louis Stevenson later called them), the Old

Town houses became increasingly shabby, overcrowded with poorer people from the country who came to find work in the town. In the end they degenerated into disease-ridden slums. The New Town, with its broad streets, elegant crescents and imposing terraces, on the other hand, was too spaciously laid out for the Old Town's relatively class-free friendliness to be carried over into it. A chilling sense of social division gradually crept into Edinburgh life. Sharing a single turnpike stair, it was impossible for Old Town people of different ranks not frequently to encounter each other, a dancing-master perhaps having to flatten himself against the wall to allow a behooped duchess to squeeze past. In the New Town a dancing-master and a duchess would rarely meet, except in the roles of employee and employer. With social segregation, the growth of the finance houses and the inevitable expansion of the city's legal and administrative machinery, Edinburgh soon gained its reputation for being 'east windy, west endy' – in Edinburgh, as in most towns, the west was the better residential area, as it was less likely that factory smoke would blow there with the prevailing wind.

Topham, in a much-quoted passage, had observed the effects of the Edinburgh winds on the New Bridge, '... which by being thrown over a long valley that is open at both ends, and particularly from being balustraded on each side, admits the wind in the most charming manner imaginable ... you receive it with the same force as you would do, were it conveyed to you through a pair of bellows.' He '... had the pleasure of adjusting a lady's petticoats which had blown almost entirely over her head, and which prevented her disengaging herself from the situation she was in'.

In 1799 one of the earliest professional guide-book writers, the Honourable Sarah Murray, found positive benefit in the high winds: 'The violent gusts of wind, continually to be felt in the streets of Edinburgh, are, I imagine, owing to its situation; and must be the cause of health to its inhabitants (they are very healthy); for had not the atmosphere of that city some powerful refiner, such as a constant high wind, it would, by its nauseous scents, poison the race of beings in it.'

By 1799 James Craig's New Town, begun in 1768, was still in course of construction. Mrs Murray thought the South Bridge 'very wide, with handsome shops on each side, except over the arch'. She commented on the North Bridge's being thrown over 'the dry trench to the New Town', the Nor' Loch having been drained before building began. She found Robert Adam's new university 'at a stand for want of money'. The original Princes Street, soon to become the victim of Victorian and later hotch-potching, seemed to her 'a noble street, a north row of houses, looking over the dry trench up the backs of the houses in the old town'. There must still have been some raw feeling of a building site about the New Town, for Mrs Murray noted: 'There cannot be much passing and repassing in the new town in summer, for in almost every street the grass grows.'

While she was too lady-like to say whether or not 'the Flowers of Edinburgh' affected her (though she does tell us that people in the middle of the street were not exempt from a splashing), she relates how she was '... one fine evening walking up the *inviting* [her italics] Canongate, nicely dressed, in white muslins.... An arch boy eyed me, and laid his scheme; for when I arrived opposite a pool, in the golden gutter, in he dashed a stone, and, like a monkey, ran off chuckling at his mischief.' When one reflects upon what made the gutter golden, it is easy to appreciate Mrs Murray's annoyance.

Holyroodhouse was then occupied by French royalty, headed by the Comte d'Artois, refugees from the Terror across the water. Mrs Murray looked down upon their residence when, energetically, she climbed the Calton Hill, from which she thought the view unsurpassable, Arthur's Seat and Salisbury Crag.

William and Dorothy Wordsworth visited Edinburgh on the way home from their Highland Tour of 1814. Dorothy recorded an impressionistic account of how the City appeared to them from Arthur's Seat:

> The Castle rock looked exceedingly large through the misty air; a cloud of black smoke overhung the city, which combined with the rain and the mist to conceal the shapes of the houses – an obscurity which added much to the grandeur of the sound that proceeded from it. It was impossible to think of anything that was little or mean, the goings-on of trade, the strife of men, or every-day city business: – the impression was one, and it was visionary; like the conceptions of our childhood of Baghdad or Balsara when we have been reading the Arabian Nights' Entertainments. Though the rain was very heavy we remained upon the hill for some time, then returned by the said road by which we had come, through green flat fields formerly the pleasure-grounds of Holyrood House, on the edge of which stands the old roofless chapel, of venerable characteristic.

The year 1819 turned out to be a good one for comment on Edinburgh. Sir Walter Scott's son-in-law and biographer John Gibson Lockhart accurately defined the station and situation of the place just four years after Waterloo: 'Here is the capital of an ancient, independent and heroic nation, abounding in buildings ennobled by the memory of illustrious deeds of good and evil; and in others, which hereafter will be reverenced by posterity, for the sake of those that inhabit them now. Above all, here is all the sublimity of situation and scenery – mountains near and afar off – roads and glens – and the sea itself, almost within hearing of its waves.'

Another poet, also better known as a biographer (in this case of Nelson), Robert Southey, arrived in the city later that same year. He came to Edinburgh to begin an extensive tour of roads, harbours and bridges with the great engineer Thomas Telford. Southey stayed at McGregor's Hotel in Princes Street. He spent his first day in the city calling on friends and relations and on the publisher Blackwood, who gave him a copy of Lockhart's newly published book, *Peter's Letters to his Kinsfolk*. 'The view from his hotel in the morning,' wrote Southey, 'when the fires are just kindled, is probably the finest smoke-scape that can anywhere be seen. Well may Edinburgh be called Auld Reekie! and the houses stand so one above another, that none of the smoke wastes itself upon the desert air before the inhabitants have derived all the advantage of its odour and smuts. You might smoke bacon by hanging it out of the window.'

Southey spent a day or two exploring Edinburgh. He thought odd and characteristic the High Street wynds, '... down which an English eye may look, but into which no English nose would willingly venture, for stinks older than the Union are to be found there'. He was also critical of the New Town's 'enormous lengths of the streets ... where there is neither protection nor escape from the severe winds to which Edinburgh is exposed' – thus anticipating Stevenson's later complaint about the New Town's 'draughty parallelograms'. In Holyrood, he opined that, while Mary, Queen of Scots, was thought beautiful by Scottish standards, '... anywhere else such a countenance would only be called good-looking and that rather by courtesy than by right.'

A more fruitful visit was to be paid to Holyrood in 1829, when, in early August, the young Mendelssohn visited it: 'In the evening twilight we went today to the palace where Queen Mary lived and loved; a little room is shown there with a winding staircase, leading up to the door. Up this way, they came and found Rizzio in that little room, pulled him out, and three rooms off there is a dark corner, where they murdered him. The chapel close to it is now roofless; grass and ivy grow there; and at the broken altar Mary was crowned Queen of Scotland. Everything around is broken and mouldering, and the bright sky shines in. I believe I found to-day in that old chapel the beginnings of my Scotch Symphony.'

The Danish master of the fairy-tale (though he is revered in his own country for much else besides) Hans Christian Andersen visited Edinburgh in 1847. He came as the guest of the banker Baron Hambro, but it was Sir James Simpson, the discoverer of chloroform, who was to be his guide in the High Street, where, in the side streets, '... narrow, filthy and with six-storyed houses ... poverty and misery seem to peep out of the open hatches, which normally serve as windows, and rags and tatters are hanging out to dry'. Though he enjoyed Sir James's hospitality, and meeting such literary luminaries as John Wilson ('Christopher North') and Lord Jeffrey, he disliked the New Town, with its 'straight roads and uninteresting modern buildings' where '… one line cuts another or runs parallel to it'. He thought there was nothing more Scots about it than the fact that it had regular squares, just like the Scots plaid. It was the Edinburgh of Scott's Waverley Novels for which he reserved his warmest praise, enthusing, '… the whole of the old town is like a mighty commentary on the great works which are read in all lands.'

Restoration and Renaissance

Edinburgh has always had little enough in the way of industry compared with Glasgow, and so to a large extent it has been isolated from the evils that befell the industrial powerhouse of the west. The capital had its share of overcrowding, its waves of cholera and malaria and its hordes of escapees from poverty into drink, but to nothing like the same extent as Glasgow. Edinburgh, on the other hand, more than shared with the rest of Scotland the various schismatic movements that, even after the fundamental breakaway from Roman Catholicism in 1560, continued to fragment the Reformed Church. In 1843 Dr Thomas Chalmers led a host of 470 clergymen out of the General Assembly of the Church of Scotland to found the Free Church of Scotland in protest against, amongst other things, the custom of lairdly patronage; the largest and most influential of those schismatic movements which were to peel off throughout Victorian times until the beginning of a come-together was achieved with the union of the two main Reformed Churches in 1929.

Between 1850 and 1900 the built-up area of the city more than doubled, houses extending north to Leith and Newhaven, west to Murrayfield and south to Blackford Hill. Although by the standards of much of what was to be put up throughout the early and middle years of the twentieth century, these Victorian suburbs achieved a reasonable standard of design and construction, a very different view of them was taken in 1878 by Robert Louis Stevenson:

Day by day, one new villa, one new object of offence, is added to another; all around Newington and Morningside, the dismalest structures keep springing up like mushrooms; the pleasant hills are loaded with them, each impudent is spotted in its garden, each roofed and carrying chimneys like a house. And yet a glance of an eye discovers their true character. They are not houses; for they are not designed with a view to human habitation, and the internal arrangements are, as they tell me, fantastically unsuited to the needs of man.... They belong to no style of art, only to a form of business much to be regretted.

In spite of such elegant disapproval, Edinburgh continued to expand, however, so that its inhabitants had to be housed somewhere. Stevenson perhaps also overlooked the fact that, while the builders of the New Town were relatively more conscious of architectural standards, as construction spread down hill to the north, the houses for the less wealthy and less grand had fewer amenities and were unquestionably also financed speculatively as 'a form of business'.

Although Edinburgh has had a brewing tradition since medieval times, the Victorian years saw her manufactures increasing to produce whisky, flour, meal, biscuits, anaesthetics, cloths and yarns. She maintained her reputation as a centre for fine printing and, to some extent, publishing, though the drift south, illustrated by the establishment of the publishing house of John Murray in London's Albemarle Street early in the century, continued almost to our own day.

Though disease and drunkenness ravaged the Old Town up to 1914, the invention of chloroform by Hans Andersen's guide, Sir James Young Simpson, whose home was in Queen Street, was indicative of Edinburgh's medical achievement. Though Graham Bell went to Canada and America to invent the telephone, he was originally an Edinburgh man, as was one of the greatest of the Victorian physicists, Clerk Maxwell, though he refused a position with his own university to make his scientific contribution from Cambridge and London.

Literary life in Edinburgh during the latter half of the nineteenth century was crowned by Stevenson, though ill-health drove him away from the icy winter blasts he had endured during his childhood in Heriot Row, to the warmer breezes of a South Sea island. As a young man, he found the spiritual atmosphere of Edinburgh almost as hostile to the imagination as was the climate to his frail body. In one mood, when a young man, he saw himself as a kind of reincarnated Robert Fergusson: 'O my sighings after romance,' he complained; 'O the weary age that will not produce it.'

I walk the street smoking my pipe
And I love the dallying shop-girl
That leans with rounded stern to look at fashions;
And I hate the bustling citizen,
The eager and hurrying man of affairs, I hate,
Because he bears his intolerance writ on his face

And every movement and word of him tells me how much he hates me.

I love the night in the city,
The lighted streets and the swinging gait of harlots.
I love cool pale morning,
With only here and there a female figure,
A slavey with lifted dress and the key in her hand,
A girl or two at play in a corner of waste-land
Tumbling and showing her legs and crying out to me loosely.

For a time, escape was to be found in the pose of velvet-jacket bohemianism, until he discovered 'the romance of the bright picturesque image'. The Stevenson of *Weir of Hermiston*, however, had no need for romantic escape devices. He saw Scotland whole and had come to artistic terms with her.

Edinburgh also produced Sir Arthur Conan Doyle, but Sherlock Holmes's Baker Street had little to do with Edinburgh's New Town, on whose fringes Conan Doyle was born.

It was really through architecture and painting that the Edinburghers of Victorian times made their most confident statements. Most of the great Scottish nineteenth-century architects left some impress on the fabric of the city. Sir Henry Raeburn, painting in his studios in York Place, not only caught the last of the clan chieftains in their full colourful traditional Highland plumage but recorded the Scottish face with an intensity and veracity similar to that which the greater and more broadly gifted Rembrandt bestowed upon his fellow Dutchmen.

The single most important innovation to affect Edinburgh – as, indeed, it affected the whole of Europe and beyond – was the invention and introduction of the passenger railway. Suddenly life speeded up and distance contracted. There had been no invention of comparable significance since man discovered the wheel, life in the intervening centuries having been geared more or less to the pace of the horse.

A glimpse has come down to us of the old pre-railway life as it affected James Meikle, a clerk with the Scottish Provident Institution who eventually became President of the Faculty of Actuaries in Edinburgh. He recalled in old age the conditions under which he began his apprentice life:

I remember well the first day I entered my late office – it was the 21st October, 1839. I climbed to the top of a high stool, and my first duty was to fill up a referee's letter. The conditions of work were very different in these days from what they are now. The hours were from 10.00 to 4.00 and from 7.00 to 9.00, but it was after 10 o'clock at night and occasionally 11, before the day's work was over. There was no such thing as copying letter books then. There were no messengers ... the apprentices had to carry all the parcels to the 'Black Bull' inn, from where the mail coach to London started....

Improved communications changed the pace of business as well as domestic life when on 21 February 1842 the line from Glasgow to Haymarket was opened by the Edinburgh & Glasgow Railway Company. The Nor' Loch, which lay in the gully between the foot of the castle rock and what is now Princes Street, had, of course, been drained during the building of the first phase of the New Town. Now Trinity College Church, which stood on the site of what became the North British Hotel, was demolished to make way for Waverley Station, named after Scott's novels and opened in 1846. It was extended in 1869 and again in 1873, before being rebuilt completely at the end of the century, when it became the largest rail terminal outside London. The earliest train journeys from Edinburgh to London involved crossing the Tweed by ferry and, until 1847, travelling from Berwick to Newcastle by stage-coach, the final rail link-up between the two capitals not being connected until 1849, when Robert Stephenson's Royal Border Bridge was opened.

While the establishment of a daily rail link with London not only helped those who travelled on business but encouraged others to travel because they wanted to, it also inaugurated Edinburgh's long decline into provincialism. The slowness and discomfort of coach travel and travel by sea had to some extent enforced the expending and exploitation of the city's energies within its own bounds. Glasgow city life continued to be energized by the international nature of its order books in the shipbuilding and other heavy industries of the west; Edinburgh developed more slowly and remained frostily professional and middle class in its outlook. Increasingly, the Old Town festered in stagnant history.

While Edinburgh has never lacked its detractors, many of them from Glasgow, it has probably also evoked more poetic encomiums than any other city in northern Europe. Among the most effective of these is by Kilmarnock-born Alexander Smith, the 'spasmodic' poet who ended his relatively brief life as secretary to Edinburgh University.

The quick life of today sounding around the relics of antiquity, and overshadowed by the august traditions of a Kingdom, make residence in Edinburgh more impressive than residence in any other British city.... What a poem is that Princes Street! – the puppets of the busy, many-coloured hour move about on its pavements, while across the ravine Time has piled up the Old Town ridge on ridge, grey as a rocky coast washed and worn by the foam of centuries; peaked and jagged by gable and roofs; windowed from basement to cope; the whole surmounted by St Giles's airy crown. The New is looking at the Old. Two Times are brought face to face and are yet separated by a thousand years. Wonderful are winter nights when the gully is filled with darkness and out of it rises, against the sombre blue and the frosty stars, that mass and bulwark of gloom, pierced and quivering with innumerable lights.

Just as Edinburgh's cholera epidemics were less devastating than those which all but engulfed Glasgow, so the Victorian trade recessions hit the western megalopolis much harder than the capital. Thus after the 1914–18 war Edinburgh was less affected by the decline of the twenties and the slump of the thirties.

As Edinburgh prospered and spread its suburbs over the surrounding countryside, its heritage was increasingly neglected. Altered post-war fortunes resulted in divided houses and the creeping spread of offices into the New Town. The Old Town continued to rot.

The Victorian scholar George Birbeck Hill visited Edinburgh in the late 1880s and penetrated one of the courts off the Lawnmarket. He found it difficult for the stranger

... who passes from the thronged street under the low archway into that quiet, but gloomy, and even shabby-looking court, to picture to himself the gay and lively company which once frequented it. Now ragged, bare-footed children are playing about; in some of the windows there are broken and patched panes of glass, while high above one's head, from the different storeys, are hanging out to dry garments of various sorts and hues, on a curious kind of frame-work, let down by a pulley and string, till it stands out square from the wall. Some of the houses are coloured with a yellow wash; in others the stones round the windows and at the corners are painted red. The uncoloured stone is grey darkened by years of smoke. The lower windows are guarded by iron gratings.

My kindly ersatz-uncle, Doan (so called because, as a very young child, I could not say John), who acted as a kind of surrogate father to me during my infant years, while my real father was recovering from a serious jaw-wound sustained in France in 1918, took me wandering in and about the High Street of Edinburgh when I was about twelve or thirteen. Coming from what would now be called a prosperous professional middle-class home, it was my first introduction to the sight and smell of poverty. I have never forgotten the experience.

During the 1939–45 war, the decay of the Old Town accelerated. Destruction and replacement rather than restoration were the first thoughts of the earliest mandatory local authority planners in the immediate post-war years. Indeed, one or two houses were either taken down or fell down through lack of maintenance. Prowling around wynds and courts in the late forties, I saw what Hill had seen half a century earlier, and recorded the double experience in a poem (revised in later years), which is certainly not out of place here.

Warriston's Close, Halkerston's Wynd,
crookit and cramped, dim, drauky, blind … [damp

High-heapit tenements, lair on lair,
squeezan the licht tae a narra gair; [strip

glaur mair auld nor the stanes themsels [mud
gether't in dubs roun court-yaird wells; [puddles

doorways and drains that swalla smells, [swallow
bluntit as tane wi tither mells; [one mixed with
another

widdies raxan at wind-flaucht air, [gallows reaching
claes wi'oot bodies dancan there; [wind-blown
[clothes

lawyers hurryan up and doun
frae posher hames in the newer toun;

shoppers aff tae the braw bazaars
o Princes Street in their brun tramcaurs;

kerbside shawlies cryan for sale
cockles and winkles frae the pail;

auld wives skreichan at shilpit weans,
rickets and history in their banes;

gloaman pubs whaur a frienly stour [twilight
shauchles aroun each bricht-lit door; [shuffles

the whup-like edge of wir Lallans leed [whip tongue
flick't roun a guilty guideman's heid.

Warriston's Close, Halkerston's Wynd,
where puir folk wantit while judges dined …

wemen o pleisure, aulder nor years,
whingean wanchancey worn-oòt leers;   [unlucky; looks

Ramsay, Fergusson, Mary, Knox
thocht less o noo than fear o the pox;

Fegs, and your gey romantic places
for thae wha ainly pree your faces.   [experience

The between-the-wars council houses Edinburgh built round its
environs – particularly the vastly depressing Niddry Estate – were
probably no worse than similar agglomerations put up by Glasgow
and Dundee, though one might perhaps reasonably have looked for
better. Nor did Edinburgh's post-1939–45 new housing, at least until
comparatively recently, suggest any sort of qualitative kinship with the
building of its New Town. Yet during this period after the Second
World War (a time of frequently somewhat unfortunate architectural
innovation, government cutbacks and use of untested building
materials) a new appreciation of the superb workmanship and design
of the Georgian town emerged. Edinburgh was suddenly recognized
as being an architectural exemplar by European standards.

Following a house-by-house voluntary survey over a period of two
years, and an international conference held thereafter in the
eighteenth-century Assembly Rooms in June 1970, a remarkable
exercise in community enterprise was organized by The Scottish Civic
Trust in conjunction with the Edinburgh Architectural Association. It
resulted in the setting-up of the Edinburgh New Town Conservation
Committee under the chairmanship of a former lord provost and with
its own architect-director and staff, funded jointly by government and
local authority. The Edinburgh New Town Conservation Committee
has since been steadily engaged in a modest but ongoing programme
of essential restoration, a task likely to prove demanding for many a
decade to come.

Today, all but a few of the noble New Town houses have been
divided into flats, albeit in the grander parts luxurious ones. Even the
former air of New Town stuffiness has largely gone, only the ghost of
it perhaps lingering on a wintry Sabbath. Many of those who were
brought up in the New Town remember its sights and sounds
affectionately, none more so than Moray MacLaren, recalling a
pre-First World War New Town childhood:

Let it not be thought, however, that the present chronicler smiles (if he smiles at all) in anything but affectionate remembrance of that now half-forgotten world in which the houses of the New Town really were houses. He recalls with nostalgia that is not wholly sentimental those vast green doors at the top of a wide flight of steps, the bell-pull, long and solid, framed in a wider square of gleaming and always polished brass, the number of the house standing out also in bold and equally new polished brass Roman figures upon the woodwork of the door. He remembers how, when the door was opened to him by a maid in stiff starched linen, he was admitted into a hall which, to his childish eyes, seemed as large and as dark as a church. He remembers the size of the hat rack, of the press for the men's overcoats, the huge round dinner gong standing by the stair, whose polished surface caught and reflected only the most transient gleams of Edinburgh daylight. He remembers the dining-room to the right of the hall, again huge, brown and ill-lit, with dark curtains over the enormous windows. He sees once more that long dining-table of dully gleaming mahogany, capable of being lengthened even more by the insertion of flaps so that it could seat twenty of a family at Christmas time, New Year, or upon reunions. It is a room which to him recalls domestic devotion as much as domestic festivity; for it was here, every morning, that family prayers were held.

How vividly the memory of those large Edinburgh New Town family prayers return to mind. Daily domestic devotions were of course not uncommon at that time in Scotland, and even in England – though it is true that in the first decade of this century the custom was on the decline – but surely few family prayers elsewhere could have acquired quite the rich and solemn ceremonial of those held in the dining-rooms of the New Town. Himself the head of the family would be seated at the end of the table nearest the huge curtained windows. On either side, flanking him in crescent form, were the members of his family, his wife on his right hand, his eldest daughter on his left, and at the ends of the crescent were the children. When the family was seated, a bell was rung, and the servants trooped in in reverse order of seniority, the butler or manservant (if there was one) bringing up the rear, marching his female brood before him like a barnyard fowl with his hens. There would be the solemn reading of God's word; then, upon the injunction 'Let us pray' there would be a scraping of chairs, a susurration of skirts, and the whole company of twenty or more would, with one exception, turn, kneel, and bury their faces in the chairs on which they had been sitting. The one exception was the head of the house. He, still seated, would but bend his head over the open Bible on the table before him and, with clasped hands and closed eyes, address our Creator on behalf of his family and his servants in the New Town of Edinburgh. Permeating the atmosphere, like incense in a cathedral, there was the scent of sausages, bacon, fresh coffee and old leather. How evocative, even now, is that combination of almost forgotten smells.

A poet of the 1930s for whose work I have long had an affection, Ruthven Todd, the only Scottish member of the Auden-Spender-Day Lewis group, vividly recorded his Edinburgh childhood. He recalled his 'city of grey stone and bitter wind', the 'place where dry minds grow crusts of hate, as rocks grow lichens'; above all, the tenements 'sooted up with lying history'.

Knox spoke sweetly in the Canongate – 'I was not cruel
To gaunt Mary, the whore denying the hand that lit the fuse.'
Charles Stuart returned, alive only to the past, his venture
That was little but a dream, forgetting the squat bottle,
Quivered in the lace-veined hand and the unseeing sharpness of his
    eyes.
Bruce could not stir the cobwebs from his skeleton,
And the editor spoke regretfully, but firmly to poor Keats.

Here the boy Rimbaud paused, flying love and lust,
Unnoticed on his journey to the Abyssinian plains
And the thick dropsy of his tender leg. Here the other Knox,
Surgeon and anatomist, saw the beauty of the young girl
Smothered by Burke and Hare. And here, O certainly,
God was the private property of a chosen few
Whose lives ran carefully and correctly to the grave.

This, deny it as I like, is still my city and these ghosts,
Sneer as I may, have helped to make me what I am.
A woman cried in labour and Simpson inhaled his vapour
Falling anaesthetized, across the drawing-room table.
John Graham, laird of Claverhouse, did not have tears
For those he killed, nor did the silver bullet weep for him.
This city, bulwark of the eastwind, formed me as I am.

Architecture and painting make public statements but do not necessarily expose their creators to face-to-face public criticism. Until recently, the Scots have felt much more comfortable in the private rather than the public arts; their excellence has been in writing and painting rather than in producing plays or composing operas, where the creator has to come out into the open. Though the Scottish colourists of the early twentieth century, Peploe, Hunter and Cadell, really had their roots in Glasgow and the West rather than in Edinburgh, the neo-colourists of the post Second World War years – Anne Redpath, Ian Fleming, Robin Philipson and others – certainly made their mark. Indeed, the distinguished art critic Eric Newton observed that during the fifties and sixties there was often more to enjoy and be excited by in the annual exhibitions of Edinburgh's Royal Scottish Academy than in those of London's Royal Academy.

By then, of course, the Edinburgh International Festival of Music and Drama, founded in 1947, not only had been successfully launched but was approaching the height of its flowering as the finest and most comprehensive general festival of the arts in the western world. Sadly, 'east windy, west endy' remained the attitude of many Edinburgh people to their festival, despite the point that it was also a commercial success which brought millions of extra pounds to the city over the years. As I have already observed, four decades on, the festival appears to be somewhat in decline, its scope much curtailed, its quality more variable and its premier status no longer unchallengeable.

In the early years it provoked the caustic wit of one of Edinburgh's raciest poets, Robert Garioch, in 'Embro to the Ploy'. The military tattoo, held annually on the castle esplanade, is, of course, one of the festival's most popular, if least cultural, events.

> When day's anomalies are cled
> in decent shades of nicht,
> the Castle is transmogrified
> by braw electric licht.
> The toure that bields the Bruce's croun   [shelters
> presents an unco sicht
> mair sib to Wardour Street nor Scone,   [related
> wae's me for Scotland's micht,
>   says I
> in Embro to the ploy.

There are the church halls and other unlikely places turned into temporary theatres; the pubs suddenly filled with

>   ... orra folk   [odd people
> whaes stock-in-trade's the scrievit word,   [written
> a twicet-scrievit joke.   [twice-written
> Brains, weak or strong, in heavy beer,
> or ordinary, soak....

Finally,

> They toddle hame doun lit-up streets   [stagger
> filled wi' synthetic joy;
> aweill, the year brings few sic treats
> and muckle to annoy.   [much
> There's monie hartsom braw high-jinks   [many hearty
> mixed up in this alloy   pranks
> in simmer, when aa sorts foregether
> in Embro to the ploy.

Garioch was part of what Eric Linklater called the 'Second Wind' of the literary movement known as the Scottish Renaissance, grouped around the poet Hugh MacDiarmid and the song writer Francis George Scott. While not directly based in Edinburgh, Garioch apart, the city produced, or adopted, Norman MacCaig and Sydney Goodsir Smith. Smith, like Garioch, owed some kinship to Fergusson. Smith's masterpiece 'Under the Eildon Tree' imagines aloof, dignified Edinburgh indulging in a basic human activity common to all mankind:

The lums o the reikan toun
Spreid aa ablow, and round
As far as ye could leuk
The yalla square o winnocks
Lit ilkane by a nakit yalla sterne
Blenkan, aff, syne on again,
Out and in and out again
As the thrang mercat throve,
    The haill toun at it
Aa the lichts pip-poppan
    In and out and in again
        I' the buts and bens
        And single ends,
            The banks and braes
    O' the toueran cliffs o lands,
Haill tenements, wards and burghs, counties,
    Regalities and jurisdictiouns,
        Continents and empires
        Gien ower entire
Til the joukerie-poukerie!
Hech, sirs, whatna feck of fockerie!
Shades o Knox, the hochmagandie!
    My bonnie Edinburrie,
        Auld Skulduggerie!
Flat on her back sevin nichts o the week
Earnan her breid wi her hurdies' sweit.

Norman MacCaig is concerned with the ghosts of history

Across this gulf where skeins of duck once clattered
round the black Rock and now a tall ghost wails
over a shuddering train, how many tales
have come from the hungry North, of armies shattered
and the old cause won, a useless battle lost,
a head rolled like an apple on the ground;
and Spanish warships staggering West and tossed
on frothing skerries; and a king come to be crowned.

Look out into this brown November night
the smells of herrings from the Forth and frost;
the voices humming in the air crossed
more than the Grampians; East and West unite,
in dragony swirlings over the city park,
their tales of death and treacheries, and where
a tall dissolving ghost shrieks in the dark
all history greets you with a Bedlam stare.

Today, Edinburgh is still the seat of the Scottish Office, established in 1885 and ever since the Scottish centre of London-based government. David Hamilton's splendid classical Royal High School, on the eastern slopes of the Calton Hill, was redesigned in 1979 to house a devolved Scottish Assembly for Scottish affairs, voted out by a dubiously devised Referendum in 1979. Yet every poll taken during the 1980s suggests that the majority of Scots still desire such a reorganization in the governing of Britain. As and when Edinburgh once again becomes a *de facto* rather than a *de jure* seat even of devolved government, perhaps it may slough off its air of provincialism and manifest once again a more robust indigenous intellectual and cultural homogenity. Meanwhile the man-made heritage of the past upon which its reputation largely rests remains a glorious one and at last, after too many decades of being taken for granted and neglected, is being lovingly protected and conserved.

In the earliest of the photographs that form the second section of this book, Edinburgh's character and sense of identity seem perhaps stronger than in the more urbane photographs representing our here-and-now. If that distant Past certainly produced a less hygienic, more leisurely way of life among buildings often externally little altered, at least our perplexing Present produces a stronger and infinitely more urgent challenge. Even in this there is continuity, for it is a challenge that has altered little since Stevenson diagnosed it more than a century ago: 'Edinburgh has but partially abdicated and still wears, in parody, her metropolitan trappings. Half a capital and half a country town, the whole city leads a double existence; it has long trances of the one and flashes of the other.... It is half alive and half a monumental marble.'

For which will it finally settle?

Edinburgh
and the
Photographers

2

A Panorama

Long before photography, it was recognized that Edinburgh was a strikingly beautiful city, but its strength was in its setting rather than in the attractiveness of individual buildings. Certainly before the construction of the New Town it could not be said that there was much 'beauty' in evidence within the medieval walls. 'Picturesque' would have been a polite description for the lands and closes. Quite what an imaginary documentary photographer would have found to photograph on the Royal Mile of the sixteenth century scarcely bears contemplating, but the distant view would have been another matter.

Even today, the remote views of Edinburgh are among its best. No matter from which direction you approach the city, and however often, it is always able to catch your eye and your attention. The approach by air from the south-east is especially spectacular and must account for miles of film exposed by those lucky enough to have a window seat, but the roads to Edinburgh from all directions have their particular spots which invite a pause at least, if only the traffic will allow. Even the arrival by rail, traditionally the least favoured visual approach to a city, provides glimpses of what is to come. There is a special bonus of the sudden release from subterranean gloom to discover the dramatic base of the Calton Hill or the castle itself.

The sweep of the coast, of the line of the Old Town down the Royal Mile, the sense of space and of a larger context of the hills and the Firth of Forth are not entirely to the photographer's benefit perhaps. The urge is to capture the width, the general, not the particular, and we know how disappointing the results of trying to take in too much can be. Standing on the castle ramparts or on the top of Arthur's Seat, the Braids, Blackford or Calton Hill, the need is for something that will complement the scale of the view, and sooner or later the word 'panorama' presents itself. Significantly, that word has a special meaning in relation to Edinburgh. In fact, Edinburgh can claim to have given currency to the expression and birth to one of photography's most popular precursors.

In 1787 an Irish portrait-painter, Robert Barker (1739–1806), patented a new invention. The idea was really an extension of the trend to produce paintings on a monumental scale (not unlike the twentieth-century cinema equivalents) and to charge the public admission for the thrill. What made Barker's idea patentable was that the painting wrapped around the viewer, in a full 360-degree circle. It was, in fact, the world's first 'panorama' and the predecessor of all the panoramas, dioramas, cycloramas, myrioramas throughout the world that were to be the delight and fascination of the Victorian age and which were only finally dislodged in their last and more sophisticated forms by the coming of cinema itself.

Robert Barker's first panorama, 'View of Edinburgh', depicted the scene from the Calton Hill. Initially, it does not seem to have been a great success. Perhaps the reality outside the panorama overwhelmed the artefact. Perhaps, more likely, the Edinburgh public were their customary conservative selves (the first film-showing in Edinburgh had a similar fate). Whatever the cause, Barker took off for Glasgow and London, where his 'View of London' was a tremendous hit and launched him, and the whole panorama business, on the road to success and wealth.

The full glory of a panorama is a rarity these days, but there is a good example in The Hague, where Mesdag's Panorama (1881) still flourishes. There is also the extraordinary example of a semi-panorama, photographed by David Octavius Hill and Robert Adamson in the 1840s, to be found at the end of this book. It would be pushing things too far to suggest that there is any direct connection between Barker and Hill and Adamson, but panoramas as a phenomenon must have been known to Hill and Adamson (Scotland's two great early photographers, of whom more anon), and it is conceivable that they knew of Barker's – albeit his was more than a generation before.

By coincidence, 1787 also saw another birth – of the literal kind. Jacques Louis Mandé Daguerre was born on 18 November 1787 at Cormeilles-en-Parisis (he died in 1851). His career was to follow on, in a sense, from that of Barker, for Daguerre was to take the diorama towards the peak of sophistication when it and dozens of similar devices became the craze of the first part of the nineteenth century. But it is as one of the principals in the coming of photography that he figures in our story, for it was he who in 1839 first announced the 'invention' of a new medium.

There is an interesting Edinburgh connection with Daguerre. He was a fine painter not only of dioramas but of landscape in the conventional manner, and his 'Holyrood Abbey by Moonlight' hangs in the Walker Art Gallery in Liverpool. The idea of Daguerre as a tourist in Edinburgh before the invention of photography is intriguing. Did he meet the Edinburgh scientists and artists whose role in photography's first days were to be so significant? There is no reason why he should not. Many of the individuals who were to be Edinburgh's first photographers were undoubtedly around when Daguerre visited the city in the 1820s.

At any rate, it is pleasing to think of Daguerre as one of those who helped in the export of Edinburgh's image. Until the 1840s that image was always rather second-hand – and maybe not always the worse for that. But in 1839, thanks largely to Daguerre and his English opposite number William Henry Fox Talbot (1800–77), all that changed and a much more accurate representation of reality than Daguerre's moonlit ruins became possible.

The Edinburgh Connection

From the outset, Edinburgh was a natural home for the photographer. Its topography provides dramatic perspectives almost as a matter of course. The historical accidents and calculations which resulted in a castle on a mighty rock, a palace set in front of crags, an ancient thoroughfare down the spine between, a modern street from which to enjoy the cityscape, and a hill at one end perfectly suited to accommodate appropriate monuments, also threw up a society which prized intellect and enquiry, scientists and artists. So it was that Edinburgh could come to claim not only those who contributed significantly to the invention of the new art but also the first to understand and properly employ it. As Sir David Brewster (1781–1868) wrote to Fox Talbot in July 1842, 'I think you will find that we have, in Scotland, found out the value of your invention not before yourself, but before those to whom you have given the privilege of using it.'

Edinburgh in the nineteenth century certainly provided an intellectual climate ideal to foster photography, but climate of the meteorological sort has never been the city's strongest attraction. It says a lot for Edinburgh's susceptibility to the camera lens that, despite the obvious difficulties, one can observe any number of camera-wielders, amateur and professional, lining the railings of Princes Street on any day of the year (I have counted twenty on a dull November afternoon). The wind that is the price paid for the city's romantic situation proved trying for many early photographers, and their sitters, but the element which is the life of photography is light, and in that department Edinburgh offers both rich rewards and, as we shall see, an interesting historical paradox. Edinburgh's nickname 'Auld Reekie' may count for little today, but it may hold the clue to the making of many of the early images of the city.

To explain the relation between Edinburgh and the history of photography, it is necessary to begin not just at the medium's invention but many years before. Photography is unique in that it is the synthesis of scientific and aesthetic principles with results which may be used in the service of art, commerce, history, science and a host of other human applications. Photography is everywhere today, often in a multitude of guises within design, printing, film, television and so on. Its origins, however, are very ancient.

Just below the castle, at the top of the Royal Mile, stands Edinburgh's famous Camera Obscura. In its circular chamber immediately under the roof, generations of visitors have adjusted their eyes to the delicate and beautiful image on the table in front of them. It takes a second or two to register that what you see is not some artificial representation but a vision of reality, that there is movement of people, of traffic, of the branches of the trees. This is 'Nature's television', you will be told, and in the strict sense of the word – 'seeing at a distance' – that is indeed what it is. Even to a modern audience, over-familiar with television of the other kind, there is something fascinating about the experience. It is amusing to feel superior (literally) and to watch the pedestrians in the High Street unaware of their role in our entertainment. There is something close to magic in the capturing of the gentle light and colour in this dark room.

If the phenomenon of the camera obscura can still impress us today, the impact of its discovery on whoever first observed it must have been enormous. The principle that light entering a dark room through a very small hole will project onto a surface the image of whatever is in line outside was certainly known to the ancient Greeks. According to the distinguished historian of photography Helmut Gernsheim, the original application of the principle was in observing solar eclipses, but it seems that the general use had been discovered long before it was written up in detail in the fifteenth century; by the time Leonardo da Vinci was describing its usefulness to artists, it was surely very well known. With the addition of a lens and the reduction in size to a small box with the image viewed by looking in (rather than being in with it) or on a ground glass screen, the basics of the modern camera were already in place long before the chemistry was available to transform the frustratingly fleeting images provided by nature into permanent record.

To would-be artists, the elusiveness of the picture in the camera obscura must have been indeed very frustrating. However accurate their tracing of the picture on the screen, the gap between their efforts and the reality confronting them must have seemed enormous. Great artists, such as Vermeer and Reynolds, might be able to use it as merely a point of departure, a mechanical aid, to assist their own genius, but for lesser mortals the effect must have been merely tantalizing.

It was not the camera obscura, however, but a related device, the camera lucida, that was to trigger the invention of one of the two main photographic processes, the negative-positive system devised by William Henry Fox Talbot. The inadequacy of his attempts to delineate the scenes of beauty on Lake Como in 1833 led him to speculate on the means of capturing the image chemically. A long time before Fox Talbot's difficulties on Lake Como, however, the first steps had already been taken towards solving his problem.

Like so many inventions of major importance, photography was not the achievement of any single person – not Daguerre, not Fox Talbot – but rather the accumulation of an immense amount of labour, and some coincidence, attributable to scores of people and circumstances in many places and over a considerable period of time. It is true that only these two men made formal announcements of the new invention – within a few weeks of each other in 1839 – but they had arrived at different systems by different routes and were unaware of each other up to the last moment. If they had common ancestry in their inventions, it was only in their use of the camera obscura and the other, just as ancient, observation of the effect on certain substances of exposure to light. In that department of the invention, Edinburgh certainly had a stake.

The Edinburgh of the Enlightenment must have been an extraordinary place. The very idea that within such a relatively small city there should have been so many men of genius, if only for two or three decades, is surprising and exciting. Hume, Adam Smith and Walter Scott would seem more than enough to be contained by any community, but there were not only philosophers and writers on the streets but scientists as well, and it was perhaps the greatest of these, Dr Joseph Black FRS, who contributed indirectly but importantly to the invention of photography.

Scientific education in Scotland had a high international reputation towards the end of the eighteenth century, so it was natural for Thomas, the well-off son of Josiah Wedgwood, to head for Edinburgh to further his knowledge of the subject of his choice. Dr Joseph Black was famous for his lectures on chemistry, in at least one of which he discussed the effect of light on nitrate of silver. Wedgwood was at Edinburgh University from 1786 to 1788, but Black was already associated with the Wedgwood family in a circle which also included

James Watt.

Before the end of the century, Wedgwood was engaged in the work which would ensure his place and therefore Black's in the history of photography. The result was the publication in 1802 of an article in the journal of the Royal Institution entitled 'An account of a method of copying paintings upon glass and of making profiles by the agency of light upon nitrate of silver. Invented by T. Wedgwood Esq. with observations by H. Davy'. (Davy is more usually associated with the invention of the miners' lamp, but he too has an honourable place in the story.)

Sadly, these efforts came to little. The images obtained in a camera obscura were too faint and impermanent, and those made on sensitized material by direct contact could not be retained either. What they had failed to achieve was a method of fixing the image. Otherwise they were on exactly the lines that Fox Talbot used thirty years later in making his 'photogenic drawings' and 'calotypes'. Of all the 'near-misses' in the course of the discovery of photography, this one is the most painful to contemplate. 'If only ...' is an unrewarding game to play at the best of times, but it is hard not to regret the lack of good fortune that has deprived us of images of the first forty years of the nineteenth century.

There is yet another Edinburgh connection with the beginnings of photography, and a rather odd one at that. Of the remarkable Nasmyth family, Alexander is probably best known, as the painter of the most famous portrait of Robert Burns. His own connections with photography are limited to his tutorship of the young landscape painter David Octavius Hill and the fact that he owned a camera obscura, but his son, D.O. Hill's friend James, seems to have taken the new art very seriously.

James Nasmyth was to become one of the great Victorian engineers, and his 'steam hammer' one of the key inventions of the century. In June 1841 he 'rigged up out of an old Iron Box with a Spectacle Eye on the lens to explain to his wife the construction of a camera'. Given his background, we have to take seriously that in one of his notebooks, now in the National Library of Scotland on King George IV Bridge, there is a photograph on paper of a cityscape (probably Paris) by a Frenchman, Gustave Froment. Its date is 1835, four years earlier than it has any right to be. Now Nasmyth was unlikely to have got the date wrong and, as we have already seen, the technology was available if only a few connections could be made. So there is the possibility that another 'inventor' of photography has even yet to be discovered, from evidence in Edinburgh.

Certainly photographs, of sorts, had been produced before 1835 and in France. The oldest existing one is by Nicephore Niépce and dates from 1826 or 1827. Made by a process involving an eight-hour exposure of a pewter plate coated with a form of bitumen, it dimly shows the view from the photographer's window in Gras but gives little notice of the wonders that were to come in the following decades.

The two systems announced to the world, within weeks of each other in 1839, were in marked contrast. Daguerre had perfected a process which was in direct line of descent from that of Niépce. The 'daguerreotype' was a beautiful object. A polished copper plate, coated with silver, was sensitized with iodine vapour, developed with mercury vapour and fixed with a solution of common salt. The resultant image was shiny, metallic and precise in its detail. It was also a positive, with the picture laterally reversed, and was difficult to view at anything other than a very precise angle because of the mirror-like surface. Its other disadvantage was that it required a very long exposure, of many minutes. Nonetheless its advent was a sensation, and rightly so.

Fox Talbot's method was much more recognizably like the photographs of today in that his sensitized-paper process resulted in a negative from which a positive or positives could be printed by contact. His system, too, was far from perfect (he announced it only in reaction to the news from France), and it suffered the same problems of long exposure. His had the added problem that the image, though an attractive orange-brown in tone, was rather imprecise. His 'photogenic drawings' (images made by contact from leaves, lace and the like) whose invention preceded the 'Talbotype' or 'calotype', as it came to be called, were also very beautiful, but it was the sheer novelty of these 'sun drawings' that took the public by storm on both sides of the English Channel.

Fortunately the momentum of invention did not stop there. The discovery, independently by both Daguerre and Talbot, of the latent image reduced exposure times dramatically, and although it was still to be some years before sitters no longer had to hold still for at least a few seconds, by the beginning of the 1840s practical photography had fully arrived. Inevitably, there was great rejoicing, and equally great jealousies at personal and national levels were aroused.

Daguerre, honoured and rewarded by the French government, announced that he was giving his invention freely to the world, or at least to that part of the world occupied by France. Fox Talbot took out patents for England, Wales and Berwick-upon-Tweed (technically still a Scottish town occupied by England) but was advised not to bother with Scotland, advice which turned out to be crucial to the story of photography in Edinburgh. Soon amateurs and professionals, licensed or unlicensed, were at their photographic pleasure or business throughout Europe.

The new sensation had its casualties, of course. The miniaturists and silhouettists who had provided the only cheap means of acquiring a likeness of family or friend went into immediate decline. Some had the sense to join rather than fight the trend: George Washington Wilson, an Aberdonian whose career took just that dramatic swerve, proved enormously successful.

Science and Fine Art

Many of the first photographers were no doubt out to make a quick killing from the new craze, but from the very start there was a wide range of ambitions among those who took it up. Some saw it very much in terms of commerce, certainly, but there were those whose perception of photography was of a new art form, and many who saw it as an aid to the pursuit and propagation of knowledge. All three approaches were in evidence in the Edinburgh of the 1840s.

For us it is virtually impossible to look at photography with an innocent eye. Photography so pervades our daily lives, in so many guises, that to imagine seeing a photograph for the first time is as much beyond us as trying to conceive of our contemporary world without a reproduced image in sight. Photography and its allies in every form of graphic reproduction, still and moving, are everywhere we look. Photography has become so much a part of our perception of reality that we sometimes find it hard to distinguish between reality and its representation.

For those who saw the first photographs, the effect was close to miraculous. Perhaps the nearest we can get to their experience is to watch a photograph develop in the dark-room. There is certainly something special in seeing an image form itself before one's eyes, and the sense one has is of observing a natural rather than a mechanical process.

This was the aspect of photography that seems to have struck the Victorians. What many of them saw was nature, even God, at work, with man as an agent rather than creator. Such a position was consistent with a time of great discovery in science, 'natural philosophy', and it showed itself in the language in which photography was first described.

The Pencil of Nature was Fox Talbot's choice of title for the first published volume of photographs. 'Sun pictures' was a common description, and a Hill–Adamson calotype bears the inscription '*sol fecit*' – 'the sun made it' – which does less than justice to the artists concerned. 'The self-operating process of Fine Art,' said *The Spectator* on 2 February 1839. The idea that nature was, as it were, delineating herself ('impressed by nature's hand') may seem whimsical to us today, but the self-replicating phenomenon clearly was crucial to the Victorian perception of photography.

Inevitably there were groups with special interests whose reactions need not be taken to be those of the general public. The most famous of these, Paul Delaroche's sombre pronouncement, 'From today, painting is dead,' reflects something of the shock felt by artists and critics who saw their entire world about to come to an end. In fact, photography helped to redefine painting rather than destroy it.

More positive reactions were to be found elsewhere. One of the most interesting consequences of photography's invention was its effect on polite society. Photography in its infancy was no vulgar toy: it was the province of the well-educated and the well-off. One of the first demonstrations of photography in Scotland appears to have taken place at a house party at Rossie Priory, under the patronage of Lord Kinnaird, when Sir David Brewster entertained and amazed the guests.

To be properly educated, in Victorian terms, one had to have some accomplishment in the arts, and therefore it is not surprising that photography became an extension of, or substitute for, drawing (no doubt eagerly acquired by those with less developed graphic skills). Upper-class ladies could certainly pursue photography as a hobby, and some achieved great distinction, notably Julia Margaret Cameron and the Cumbernauld-born Clementina, Lady Hawarden.

The initial social status of photography is also reflected in the number of officers in the army who took up photography. There are photographs of the Crimean War, for example, by several men who were not professional photographers but military personnel.

That, however, was in the future. If society as a whole was in a sense ripe for photography, there were specific reasons why Edinburgh should become a very significant place in the medium's early history.

Edinburgh was certainly quick off the mark in photography. There are perhaps two good reasons for this, one of which, the freedom from patent restrictions, has already been mentioned. The other, however, may be the more important and may explain why the first two or three decades in the history of photography saw Edinburgh enjoy a sort of golden age for the medium in the city during which it reached heights that remain unsurpassed.

Although that other, more famous golden age for Edinburgh, the Enlightenment, had been and gone more than a generation earlier, the city was still living in its afterglow. Hume, Smith and Black had passed on, but Sir Walter Scott did not die until 1832, the university was reaching its zenith as a centre for medical education, with men such as James Young Simpson very much in evidence, and there was a large intellectual community including Henry, Lord Cockburn, Sir David Brewster and many artists, writers and scientists of distinction, who were recognized as such not merely within the confines of the city or of Scotland but internationally. In short, Edinburgh still had good connections. Progress in the arts and sciences was just as possible in Edinburgh as in London or Paris, and the flow of information on such matters was two-way.

Exactly when the first attempt was made to make a photograph in Edinburgh is uncertain, but that it took place soon after the formal announcements of January 1839 we can be fairly sure. As early as April of that year, Dr Andrew Fyfe, President of the College of Surgeons, was proposing the use of a mirror rather than a lens as the means of concentrating light in a camera. His paper 'On Photography' appeared in July in *The Edinburgh New Philosophical Journal*: serious experimentation was evidently in progress.

The photo-historian Helmut Gernsheim credits an optician, Thomas Davidson, with being the first in Edinburgh to experiment specifically with the daguerreotype, but the first professional in the field was his contemporary James Howie, who had a rooftop studio at 45 Princes Street in 1841. Howie provides us with vivid illustration of the hazards of early photography in Edinburgh. His rooftop arrangements were literally just that: his sitters had to climb three flights of stairs and a ladder to reach the open, and windy, air, where they sat among the chimneypots to have their pictures taken. An engraving of the view from the top of the Scott Monument, made a few years later, shows Howie and his customers teetering on a narrow platform high above the pedestrians in Princes Street.

Davidson's contribution to the early days was mainly technical. He made lenses and daguerreotype cameras with considerable success and supplied Howie with equipment. Howie must also be credited with the first recorded display of temperament by a photographer. Working in Princes Street Gardens on a day when a characteristic Edinburgh gale was blowing, he was faced with a sitter who complained that his top hat, on the ground, was in danger of blowing away. '– your hat,' said Howie and threw into it a weight which was used for steadying the camera during the long exposures. That stopped the hat moving but also wrecked it by making a hole in the crown.

In any account of photography in Edinburgh, however, the central place on the stage can go only to the partnership of David Octavius Hill (1802–70) and Robert Adamson (1820–48). If Edinburgh had produced no other photographers, it and Scotland would still be secure in world recognition on the strength of their work alone. It comes as a surprise and a comfort to many Scots to discover the significance of Hill and Adamson in the eyes of the rest of humanity. Recognition at home of their achievement is another matter, however, and it is worthwhile examining the paradox.

Scotland is probably not a particularly unusual small country by world standards. True, it is endowed with natural beauty and has a tradition for educating its people well – certainly well enough to make them its principal export. It has, to be sure, a slightly anomalous relationship with that other, larger part of the kingdom with which it is united, and it enjoys (and suffers from) a reputation for certain kinds of behaviour and customs of dress which it is willing to exploit for economic purposes while purporting to being embarrassed by them.

Such small countries need heroes and usually find them in their past. They also require artists, writers, musicians and the like. Scotland has done well on the writers. Burns and Scott, particularly the latter, virtually created the Scotland known both to its inhabitants and the outside world. Musicians of world class, however, have been sadly lacking to date – no Sibelius or Grieg here – and although we have the comfort of Raeburn and Wilkie, the colourists and others among the painters, perhaps only the architects Adam and Mackintosh approach the status a small country eager for international recognition would want.

Mention on page one of the international arts histories, so to speak, would seem to be out. But Hill and Adamson deliver more or less just that. No account of world photography is likely to ignore them, and there are plenty of photo-historians and critics who will argue that their work is among the greatest ever produced. Perhaps two Victorian photographers are an unlikely pair of heroes for a small country to be asked to celebrate, but 'heroes' is what I once heard them called at a public lecture in London; maybe it is not our style, but it doesn't really excuse the Scots for the scant attention we give them and their extraordinary contribution to photography.

Hill and Adamson

The story of Hill and Adamson is certainly a remarkable one. It has in it elements which give it a peculiarly Victorian flavour, but it is more importantly an Edinburgh story with its roots in the capital's mix of science, religion and politics. It begins, however, not in Edinburgh but to the north, in another ancient university town, St Andrews.

Sir David Brewster, though certainly part of Edinburgh's intelligentsia and later principal of Edinburgh University, was at this time, the late 1830s and early forties, principal of the United Colleges of St Salvator and St Leonard in the University of St Andrews. He was recognized as a great man of science, particularly in the field of optics, and it was in that capacity that he was an associate of the inventor of one of the world's first two photographic systems, the English gentleman scientist and mathematician Fox Talbot. It was in correspondence with Brewster that Talbot conveyed the details of his process north of the border. Although there were plenty of initial setbacks, by May 1842 Brewster could report on, and send examples of, successful manipulation of the calotype process.

In this work Brewster was not alone. His main collaborator was Dr John Adamson, to whom must go the credit for the first proper calotypes in Scotland. Clearly the potential of the medium must have seemed very great, but it was nevertheless a bold act to launch anyone on calotyping as a career. That, nonetheless, was about to happen. John Adamson had a younger brother, Robert, whose health was deemed inadequate for more robust pursuits, and it was proposed that he train in the new art.

So it was that on 9 May 1843 Sir David Brewster was able to write to Talbot: 'Mr Adamson, of whom I have previously written to you, goes tomorrow to Edinburgh to prosecute, as a profession, the calotype. He has made brilliant progress and has done some of the very finest things both in Portrait and Landscape. His risk and outlay are considerable; and he is therefore anxious to make a good beginning. For this purpose he is desirous that you would allow him to state that he practises the art with your concurrence and countenance.'

Meanwhile, in Edinburgh, dramatic events were about to take place in Church politics. That there could be any connection between the Kirk and the course of the history of photography may seem very unlikely, but the truth is that the events of the next few weeks would have major repercussions for both. For the Kirk, the issue of the day was nothing less than where the power to appoint ministers should lie and therefore where control of the parishes throughout the nation really belonged – with the congregations or with those who owned the land.

Edinburgh is a good city for protest. The disposition of public spaces, halls and churches for meeting in, streets for marching in, indeed several of the attributes which make it good for photography make it ideal for processions and demonstrations, as the mob in earlier centuries discovered. The happenings of Thursday 18 May 1843 must therefore have been impressive to the onlooker, let alone the participant. If the outward appearances were dramatic, they only reflected the spiritual and political turmoil of the event.

At about one o'clock the Church of Scotland met in General Assembly in the High Kirk of St Giles. The moderator, Dr Welsh, preached on a text from Romans 14, 'Let every man be fully persuaded in his own mind.' His purpose was to ensure that the decision to be made later in the day should be based solely on scripture. He concluded (according to *The Scotsman*) with 'a few observations as to the glorious results which might be expected to arise, at some future period, out of the difficulties in which the Church was placed'.

The Assembly then adjourned to St Andrew's Church in George Street, where Dr Welsh read a statement including these sonorous words:

> ... and we do now withdraw accordingly knowingly and solemnly acknowledging the hand of the Lord in all things which have come upon us, because of our manifold sins, and the sins of this Church and nation; but at the same time with an assured conviction that we are not responsible for any of the consequences that may follow from our enforced separation from the Establishment which we loved and prized – through interferences with conscience the dishonour done to Christ's crown, and the rejection of his sole and Supreme authority as King in his own Church.

Dr Welsh then left the Church, followed by some 200 'fathers and brethren', the majority of those present, who made their way down the hill to Tanfield Hall at Canonmills, where a crowd was already waiting to greet the 'seceders'. There the first Assembly of the Free Kirk took place, including the signing of the Act of Separation and Deed of Demission.

Today the events may seem distant. The Church of Scotland's history is full of schisms and regroupings, and its authority is not what it was. Perhaps the 'Disruption' should mean more to us now than it does, concerned as it was with matters of national identity. The rhetoric was formidable and clearly it indicated not only something of the prevailing moral tone but the excitement of what was going on.

Among those present were Sir David Brewster and the artist David Octavius Hill. The 'Disruption' was strongly supported by those in the arts, writers, scientists and students. Hill, no doubt moved by the occasion, undertook to commemorate the event in a large painting which would not only depict the general scene but show all the individual participants. It was an enormous undertaking, in several senses, not least because Hill was primarily a landscape painter and there were about 500 people present. (It was a project that would cause him enormous trouble and take him over twenty years to complete.)

What happened next is best described by Sir David Brewster, in another letter to Talbot (3 July 1843):

I got hold of the artist – showed him your calotype and the eminent advantage he might derive from it in getting likenesses of all the principal characters before they dispersed to their respective homes. He was at first incredulous, but went to Mr Adamson, and arranged with him preliminaries for getting all the necessary portraits. They have succeeded beyond their most sanguine expectations. They have taken on a small scale, groups of 25 persons in the same picture all placed in attitudes which the painter desired and very large pictures besides have been taken of each individual to assist the painter in the completion of his picture. Mr D.O. Hill the painter is in the act of entering into partnership with Mr Adamson and proposes to apply the Calotype to many other general purposes of a very popular kind.

So began what was arguably the most productive partnership in the history of photography. It was so despite the many difficulties facing anyone engaging in photography at that time, and in that climate, and despite the fact that neither man enjoyed good health. Indeed, Adamson was to survive only 4½ years. He died in January 1848 at the tragically early age of twenty-seven, but by that time the pair had produced nearly 3,000 outstanding images.

Rock House is situated on the west side of the Calton Hill just above Waterloo Place and opposite St Andrew's House, for many years the principal seat of government in Scotland. It was in the 'daylight studio' at Rock House that the bulk of Hill and Adamson's work was done, under circumstances which, though hardly ideal by today's standards, were certainly an improvement on those on Mr Howie's roof. Artificial light was a thing of the future, and the necessity for long exposures in direct sunlight must have been quite a considerable constraint but, despite the conditions, Hill and Adamson produced there what has come to be recognized as the greatest artistic achievement in early photography and certainly one of the most important of any period. To put their contribution further into perspective, it should be remembered that all their output occurred within nine years of the announcement of photography as a practical process.

Although the initial task was to record 'the fat martyrs of the Free Kirk', as Lady Eastlake rather unkindly called them, Hill and Adamson were fully alive to the potential of the new medium. There were 'crowds every day at their studio', including not only the rich and famous of the city, from the Lord Provost downwards, but also a stream of visitors from every walk of life: artists, politicians, explorers, aristocrats, musicians with their instruments, authors with their books, even a Red Indian (the first in the world to be photographed) with his tomahawk, real royalty and pretending royalty (the Sobieski

Stuarts), Highlanders and Arabs – in fact, a rich selection of Victorian life.

Fortunately Hill and Adamson did not confine their activities to the garden at Rock House and photographic portraiture, but despite the cumbersome nature of their equipment and its attendant chemistry, they did go out into the city, and sometimes beyond, in search of subjects. As a result, there are calotypes of historical as well as artistic interest of an Edinburgh which can look both familiar and strange at the same time. The tourists' favourites are there, of course – the Scott Monument and John Knox's house, White Horse Close, the Castle, Princes Street and Greyfriars' Churchyard, but so too, for example, are the ancient buildings being demolished to make way for the new Waverley Station.

The success of the partnership was apparent from the outset. The division of labour between Hill and Adamson, or rather the complementary nature of their skills, seems like the very embodiment of photography itself. Adamson provided the science, Hill the art: both were photographers. Inevitably there are arguments today as to which of them should be given the main credit for the achievement, but we know from Hill's own account that it was a genuinely collaborative affair. The title page of one of their presentation albums announces that the calotypes are 'by Mr Adamson, under the artistic direction of D.O. Hill', which means, in effect, that Adamson was in charge of the actual manipulation but that Hill set up each shot, which, given his training and profession, he proceeded to do better than any contemporary and most subsequent photographers.

Of the two, Hill is much clearer to us as a character. He was convivial, amusing, outgoing and popular. In his obituary he is described as 'singing a capital song'. Moreover, in common with most prominent people of his time, he wrote letters in quantity. Add to that his fairly frequent appearance in his own and others' photographs and we have a good sense of who D.O. Hill was.

In marked contrast, we know very little of Robert Adamson. His appearances in the calotypes reinforce the impression of the frail young man, and we are indebted entirely to others and the evidence of the photographs themselves for our account of his abilities. Quite remarkably, no letter or diary of Robert Adamson has yet come to light, and he remains a frustratingly enigmatic figure.

Perhaps the saddest thing about the shortness of the partnership's span is the knowledge that Hill and Adamson had totally unfulfilled ambitions. They intended to repeat in London what they had already accomplished in Edinburgh in making the finest portraits of the great and the good. They even had plans to travel abroad, to Nuremberg, a city, like Edinburgh, with an ancient and cultured reputation. To do so they would have needed Talbot's clearance, because of the patenting problem, and there is evidence that Adamson had been making his own and very successful improvements to the calotype system, which could in itself have presented difficulties in the relationship with the inventor. In any case, none of this was to be. Hill continued after Adamson's death to try to sell the work already made, but he became frustrated and, apart from a brief episode working with another photographer, McGlashon, he reverted to his original trade and to the secretaryship of the Royal Scottish Academy, which he had helped to found. Ironically, 130 years later that same RSA was to raise a great deal of money by selling to America calotypes taken from albums presented to the RSA by Hill himself – hardly a respectful gesture.

The relationship between the Rock House operation and Fox Talbot may well have been rather problematic. Adamson and Hill were operating quite legitimately free of patent restrictions, and only if they crossed the border was there the possibility of trouble. (In fact, there was an expedition to the British Association meeting in York at which Talbot was present.) But there seems to have been a reluctance on Talbot's part to endorse the Rock House activities which may explain why it is that, although Talbot visited Edinburgh in the course of photographing his volume *Sun Pictures in Scotland*, there is no evidence of his having sat at Rock House, surely an obvious thing for him to have done.

Of Fox Talbot's status as the inventor of the calotype, there has never been much doubt, but it is only recently that he has begun to be taken entirely seriously as a photographer in his own right. Part of the problem must be that he is inevitably compared with Hill and Adamson, whose position was already recognized, and somehow it seemed enough to have been credited with the invention without having to claim executive skill as well; but we must remember that an English gentleman of Talbot's time and social position received an education in which the sciences and the arts, far from being separately corralled, were seen as two related elements within the same general philosophy. Talbot, then, must in any case be regarded as the first distinguished photographer to visit Edinburgh, and his calotype of the nearly completed Scott Monument takes its place with the better-known images of the same subject by Hill and Adamson.

Sun and Smoke

It is generally reckoned, not least by its citizens, that one of Edinburgh's greatest glories is the hard, clear light it enjoys. In common with the other towns and cities of Scotland's eastern seaboard, the capital is at its best when its ancient stonework and rocks are seen in a low-angled sun, or when its narrow closes are briefly lit with an almost extravagant brightness at midday. Under such dramatic conditions anyone who has ever held even the simplest camera can be forgiven for feeling the great urge to freeze the moment in time. It comes as something of a disappointment, then, to realize that these conditions are not really so appropriate for photography as they would seem and that the dramatic clarity which seems so inviting to the lens can be too harsh an illumination for practical purposes.

What may be even more of a surprise is the realization that, amongst the unchanging characteristics of Edinburgh, one thing that has altered since the time of the Victorian photographers is the quality of the light itself. 'Auld Reekie' was not so named without reason. The Old Town, huddled to itself for warmth, poured its soot into the atmosphere by the ton, causing problems for the environment and population which were scarcely recognized and which were countered only in the Clean Air Acts of the mid-twentieth century. Perhaps only the pioneer photographers, acutely conscious of their need for good light, were entirely aware of the effect on Edinburgh's appearance of the output of the thousands of urban lums.

One extremely light-sensitive photographer who was certainly exercised by the problem was Thomas Keith, who, after Hill and Adamson, surely ranks as Edinburgh's greatest. Like them he occupies a very solid place in the histories and encyclopaedias of the world, and similarly his involvement in photography was fairly brief. Professionally, he was a surgeon of outstanding ability – one of those individuals who contributed greatly to Edinburgh's reputation as the centre of medical excellence – and the demands of his profession were such that photography could play only a small part in his life. Amateur though he was, his meticulous approach under trying conditions resulted in some of the best of all images of Edinburgh.

Keith employed the 'waxed paper' process, which was a subtler and more advanced form of Talbot's calotype. He made his contribution to photography in the early 1850s in pictures which were mainly of Edinburgh but which also include outstanding images of the ruins of Iona. Fortunately for posterity, Keith presented a paper to the Photographic Society of Scotland on 10 June 1856 in which he gave one of the clearest accounts of the methods and problems of the early photographer. In particular, he dealt with the question of light:

> If you were to ask me to what circumstance more than any other I attribute my success, I should say, not to any peculiarity whatever in my manipulation, or to any particular strength of the solutions I

employ, but entirely to this, that I never expose my paper, unless the light is first-rate. This I have now made a rule and nothing ever induces me to deviate from it: and I may safely say that since I attended to this I have never had a failure. You are thus saved all the annoyance and vexation and loss of time in developing pictures which you know can never turn out satisfactorily. Consequently I limit the time for taking negatives to a few weeks in the middle of summer. I sensitize my paper overnight, for in the middle of summer I am almost sure of clear mornings soon after sunrise, and most of my negatives have been taken before 7 in the morning or after 4 in the afternoon. The light then is much softer, the shadows are larger and the half tints in your picture are more perfect, and the lights more agreeable. If working during the height of the day, I prefer having partly diffused light, partly sunshine.

I am quite satisfied that the commonest cause of failure arises from the paper being exposed in bad or indifferent light especially in town, where the atmosphere is so much adulterated with smoke. I never got a good picture when there was the slightest trace of that blue haze which smoke produces between the camera and the object. If you examine the air when smoke is present, with a lens, you will see it all in a state of vibration, and as it were composed of an innumerable number of small particles.

Murray Johnston, who provided the modern photographs for this book, believed that the smoke of Auld Reekie was not altogether a bad thing, in that it took the edge off the brightness and complemented the rather slow chemistry and grain papers of the first processes. It is an interesting idea that Edinburgh's golden age of photography is in part the product of aerial pollution.

Pioneers

As new, more efficient methods of making photographs were invented, the spread of commercial photography took on epidemic proportions. Scott Archer's wet collodion system, despite its hazards, was a major step forward, technically, and it unleashed dozens of practitioners on the Edinburgh scene. The revolution in public transport created by the railways and the improved roads gave birth to tourism, and with it the market for pictures of remote, and not so remote, places – souvenirs for the visitor, something to be sent home or overseas, and admired.

Prominent among the pioneers in this field was the Aberdeen photographer George Washington Wilson. This intending painter of miniatures who jumped on the photography band-wagon with great commercial success must be given credit for several innovations, including arguably 'instant' photography, or at least for exposures short enough to freeze objects in motion. In Hill and Adamson's pictures the appearance that a street is empty is, of course, only the product of an exposure that was so long that all that registers of moving people and traffic is a ghostly blur. Washington Wilson's Edinburgh, however, is fully populated by elegant Victorians, and it was his images of the city and those from the rival firm of Valentine's of Dundee that were given the greatest distribution.

Wilson's is an interesting case. His intentions were clearly practical and commercial. Had photography not been invented, he would no doubt have been a successful miniaturist in Aberdeen. Photography enabled him to develop his commercial acumen as well as his artistic skills and establish himself as one of the first major figures in the development of photography as an adjunct to tourism. Almost inevitably his view of Scotland was shaped by the legacy of Walter Scott – 'romance' being the dominant characteristic.

The quality of his work in artistic terms was very high, at least to begin with, but as the business expanded, fewer of the images were made by him, and more of the taking of the photographs was delegated to assistants. The resultant gradual decline in the standard of work can be seen as the epitome of what happened to commercial photography as a whole. There were great opportunities for expansion fuelled by the growth of travel and tourism, and however worthy the intentions at the outset, market forces would prevail.

Wilson's work therefore illustrates a very important strand in the progress of nineteenth-century photography. Within a relatively short space of time, the making of photographs for the new market had diverged completely from making photographs for other purposes and had established its own separate practices, no less valid in themselves than any other. They were not inferior but distinct.

Wilson's family firm lasted into the twentieth century and was one of the most successful in Britain. It was not the only one of its sort. Following Hill's departure from Rock House in 1868, the studio was occupied briefly by the founder of another remarkable photographic dynasty, Thomas Annan. Annan is usually associated with Glasgow, and his *Old Closes and Streets of Glasgow* is an acknowledged masterwork. His family firm, which included the great pictorialist James Craig Annan, still flourishes in Glasgow today.

Another photographer who worked at Rock House was Archibald Burns. Although Burns, William Donaldson Clark and others may not enjoy the celebrity of Hill, Adamson or Keith, there is no doubt that they were photographers of the highest ability. Of course, the Rock House connection is more than fortuitous and there are many elements in subject and style common to those who worked there. Burns, like Annan, conducted a commissioned survey of old closes.

Clark, though an amateur photographer, had connections with D.O. Hill – he took over the Princes Street shop of Hill's brother, Alexander. Although it may be going a little far to suggest that there was a conscious effort to create a 'school' of photography in Edinburgh between the 1840s and 1860s, it is obvious that the standards of both amateur and professionals in the city were extremely high. It is doubtful if a city has ever been so well served by its photographers, and in the infancy of the medium at that.

In common with other cities and towns throughout Britain, Edinburgh saw a very rapid growth in photography as a business in the 1850s. The handful of practitioners of the previous decade had included such distinguished names of Robert Adamson, Calotypist of Calton Stairs, Ross & Thomson of 90 Princes Street, and James G. Tunny of Clerk Street. By 1859 there were almost thirty photographers listed in the street directory, and six years later it was nearly fifty. Like Annan's in Glasgow, one of these firms survives to this day. The 1865–66 listing includes 'Yerbury and Stewart of 3 Hanover Street'. Yerbury's is still very much in business.

Even after these first extraordinary years, the love-affair between Edinburgh and photography continued to thrive. In 1861 it was an Edinburgh physicist James Clerk Maxwell who introduced colour photography to the world.

More than 140 years separates the oldest and youngest photographs in this book – virtually the entire span of photography's history to date. The excitement of the first years of photography is certainly remote but there were changes and innovations for photography in the latter part of the nineteenth century which were almost as dramatic as those of the forties and fifties.

The most obvious of these was the introduction of roll film and the Kodak camera ('You press the button, we do the rest') which immediately made photography possible for everyone. Whereas previously the vast majority of the population had to be content with buying the mass-produced work of such as Washington Wilson and Valentine to place in their albums, or making an occasional visit to a photographic studio to have their portraits taken, they could now become photographers in their own right. They did so, in their millions, throughout the world. The camera thereby became as much the badge of tourism as the passport and railway ticket.

There were changes of another kind that radically affected photography's progress, and particularly its status. The divergence of photography into various strands which began early in its history continued, and among those primarily concerned with photography as a medium of artistic expression there were further divisions and distinctions. Edinburgh, with some help from Glasgow, figured in one of the most important of these. In London the group known as the 'Linked Ring', comprising the most distinguished art photographers of the day, was founded in 1892. In New York in 1902 Alfred Stieglitz founded the Photo-Secession, and with it the magazine *Camera Work*, the most important critical publication, arguably, in the history of the medium.

In these moves one of the key people was James Craig Annan, son of Thomas and therefore closely connected with D.O. Hill. (He could remember as a small boy sitting on the great man's knees) It was James Craig Annan who 'rediscovered' Hill and Adamson during the 1890s and thanks to his agency that their images found their way into *Camera Work*. His own standing as a photographer of international merit was never in doubt (though he too has suffered undue neglect in his native Scotland), and it was therefore perfectly reasonable for another distinguished photographer, Joseph T. Keiley, writing in *Camera Work* of the major exhibition in Buffalo in 1911, to say, 'By all odds the most complete and finest in every respect were the collections of D.O. Hill, J. Craig Annan and Alfred Stieglitz.' (Adamson, you will notice, is conspicuously absent. For many years his contribution was largely forgotten in favour of 'the great Scotchman', as Paul Strand calls Hill elsewhere in *Camera Work*.)

The Photo-Secessionists were a remarkable group. Under Stieglitz's leadership they sought to place photography firmly in the avant-garde of modern art. *Camera Work* was not confined to discussion and illustration of photography. Works by Matisse and Picasso, their first exposure in America, appear alongside those of Steichen, Stieglitz, Demachy, Eugene, Strand, White and the rest.

One of the most prominent was Alvin Langdon Coburn (1882–1906). His name might suggest an ancestral Edinburgh connection but in fact his forbears spelled their name 'Colburn' and had emigrated to America in the seventeenth century. They came from the village of Lacock in Wiltshire, which by splendid coincidence was also the home of Fox Talbot.

However, Coburn did indeed have an Edinburgh connection. As he wrote in his autobiography, 'I consider Edinburgh one of the most beautiful cities in the world, and Robert Louis Stevenson appreciated it as few have done.' The reference is to the edition of Stevenson's *Picturesque Notes* published in 1954, which he illustrated with twenty-three photographs taken over no fewer than forty-five years, from 1905 to 1950.

For Coburn, Edinburgh's heart was the Greyfriars Kirkyard. He did not find it a particularly sombre place but that it had rather '... a kind of charm, a serene beauty of its own which lifts it out of the commonplace, and gives it stability and character which some ancient localities seem to acquire with time and association, as difficult to explain as the mysteries of love and death and the great human emotions, but then to be discovered by the visionaries of future generations who follow in the footsteps of discerning Stevenson'.

Coburn was a great photographer of more cities than Edinburgh. His images of Edwardian London and New York contrast with the distinct character of Edinburgh in the camera. Those who photograph the big city may have a wide variety of intention and approach – Annan in the Glasgow slums, John Thomson and London street life, Coburn and the Secessionists among the New York skyscrapers – but they all confront considerable difficulties, technical and aesthetic, when they take to the street.

A Photographic Legacy

One of the first and most fundamentally erroneous conclusions about photography when it was invented was that the camera could not lie. Photography certainly deals primarily with actuality but its capacity to manipulate the truth is infinite.

It must have been a traumatic experience (*c.*1843) to see yourself in a photograph for the first time. What a mirror showed you was a lateral reversal at close range. What the camera did was to show you the right way round (though not always if it was a daguerreotype) in some sort of context and at a range determined by someone else.

If you were fortunate enough to be calotyped by Mr Hill and Mr Adamson of Rock House, you were clearly in good hands and good company. What sort of result you might obtain from Mr Howie's rooftop studio was another matter. Camera-truth was no doubt as variable then as now, and the customer (always right) would be immediately ready to blame the photographer and the apparatus if the results did not please.

What applies to people applies to cities as well. Edinburgh can look mean or handsome depending on where you point the camera, how the light is and so on. If you want the truth about a city, the camera can assist and reveal, but the photographer's intention is what counts.

'Documentary', the word coined by John Grierson, the greatest Scottish film-maker, applies as much to stills as movies. 'The creative treatment' of actuality is equally the province of the photographer as the film-maker, or journalist for that matter. It is an expression which is nowadays tainted with the expectation that whatever is called 'documentary' will be propaganda and probably boring as well. It was supposed to indicate revelation and the democratization of information.

Long before the expression was invented, there was documentary photography in the sense of photography with a purpose. Dr Barnardo published images of his charges (whom he was not averse to making look worse than they were) to raise funds. Burns in Edinburgh and Thomas Annan in Glasgow were commissioned to record the old slums which were due for demolition, in Annan's case in sharp contrast to his usual subject-matter of rural landscape.

Annan's pictures of the old closes off the High Street in Glasgow highlight a problem which we would do well to bear in mind when looking at our Edinburgh photographs – the tendency of the camera to make the commonplace glamorous. In Annan's case the issue is particularly acute. He shows pictures of people huddled together in what must have been appalling conditions. He did so, however, with such technical skill that there is little sense of distress. The viewer is tempted to see the picturesque and forget the smell.

In our own century, documentary photographers have moved to the other extreme. Weegee in the New York slums concentrated on violent crime, and he spared his viewers little or nothing in conveying the facts of street life and death. Robertson in the Crimea, Gardner (from Paisley, incidentally) in the American Civil War, and McCullin in our own time all used the camera with some degree of conscious or unconscious motive.

Our Victorian photographs of Edinburgh are therefore not merely a series of happy accidents. Each one is the product of conscious effort directed to a purpose. In this book we have tried to choose pictures which, as well as showing Edinburgh as it was more than a century ago, have genuine claims to artistic merit in their own right. Of course, some are more successful than others in this respect, and it will be unsurprising if the reader concludes that the best of them are by the better-known photographers.

It is not very easy for us to grasp the difficulties faced by the Victorian photographer, although there are plenty of contemporary descriptions which would lead you to conclude that it is miraculous that anything was ever done at all. The wet collodion process, with its requirement that much of the chemical manipulation be done on the spot, seems so messy and even dangerous to health that you wonder at its popularity.

As Murray Johnston found out in making our modern images, even today, with no need to carry a tent around with you, the photographing of Edinburgh is no easy matter, and attempting it in roughly the terms of the Victorians develops a tremendous respect for their achievement. Quite apart from manipulating the camera, the photographer still has to contend with Edinburgh's climate. The wind that tried to blow Mr Howie's sitter's hat away still swirls around the town. The sunlight is still too fleeting and uncertain, and days may go by before it is right at the right time of day.

The most dramatic and obvious changes are, of course, in the effects of another Victorian invention, the internal combustion engine. Not only do cars, buses and every kind of vehicle clog Edinburgh's famously inadequate traffic system but there is a whole range of street furniture to contend with as well. As we have seen already, the slow exposures of the 1840s may have caused the streets to appear a good deal emptier than they were, but compare their few lamp-posts with the welter, the forest, of signs in Princes Street today.

The exact replication, now, of the Victorian photographs is clearly impossible – too much has changed forever, but it is possible to use the originals as points of departure or clues to what the contemporary photographs should be. The references in Johnston's photographs to the originals embrace technique as well as content. For example, a deliberately slow shutter-speed recalls the involuntary blurring of some of the old images and is a gesture towards the past.

The idea of photographs as part of our national heritage is still a relatively new one. Only in recent years has the notion of 'value' been attached to old photographs. Undoubtedly the rise in sale-room interest in the major figures of Victorian photography, such as Hill and Adamson, has seen a transformation in their status.

In the last ten years we have seen the creation of new museums and archives, including the Scottish Photography Archive at the Scottish National Portrait Gallery. There has also been a proliferation of major exhibitions and publications devoted individually and collectively to nineteenth-century photographers. There has even been the emergence of a group of young photographers in Scotland whose consciousness of the medium includes an understanding of our photographic legacy.

Scotland, as we have observed, has not been particularly rich in visual artists. It would seem that in the medium of photography the Scots have achieved something a little out of the ordinary, and Edinburgh's role in photography's growth does not have to be a matter of purely historical interest.

The
Photographs

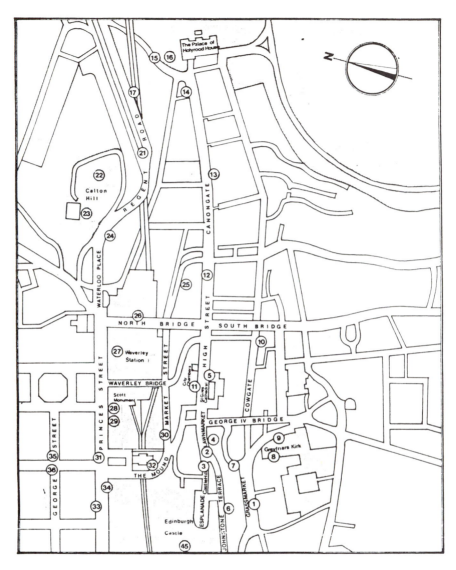

The numbers on the map represent the approximate positions from which old and new photographs of the book were taken. (The remaining locations are outside the central area shown here.) This map is not to scale.

1 The Castle from the Grassmarket

1 (a) Thomas Keith (1855), Edinburgh City Libraries

1 (b) Archibald Burns (1860s), Scottish Photography Archive

1 (c) Murray Johnston (1987)

One of the favourite photographic views of Edinburgh, perhaps because from this angle the sun favours the photographer for longer periods of the day than from Princes Street.

The Grassmarket was a fashionable residential area when first put up in the reign of James III. By Archibald Burns's time it was already fairly decayed. The Black Bull Inn is described in a guide to Edinburgh pubs as a 'comparatively new but extremely popular bar'. The date of founding of the original, shown in the older photographs, is unknown, but the *Edinburgh and Leith Post Office Directory* for 1831 lists the inn-keeper as 'Timothy Smith, Black Bull Inn, 14 Grassmarket'. This inn was demolished towards the end of the nineteenth century to make way for the Dairy Supply Company, on whose site the present pub now stands. The general Victorian dressing-up of the building of which it is part, and of the neighbouring buildings, illustrates the loss of real character which this ancient hollow, once called the Kings High Street under the Castle wall, now suffers.

1 (a)   The Castle from the Grassmarket (1855)

1 (b)   The Castle from the Grassmarket (1860s)

1 (c)   The Castle from the Grassmarket (1987)

2 Castle Hill

2 (a) Archibald Burns (1860s), Edinburgh City Libraries

2 (b) Murray Johnston (1987)

Burns's undated photograph shows to the left the former Tollbooth St John's Church, now Victoria Hall, built between 1839 and 1844 to designs by James Gillespie Graham and A.W.N. Pugin, to serve as a church for the Tollbooth and a meeting hall for the General Assembly of the Church of Scotland. The foundation stone was officially laid by Lord Frederick FitzClarence, who made a detour from the procession of Queen Victoria's state entry to the castle to do so. The Queen later noted in her *Journal* 'the oddity of laying the foundation stone to a church then nearly completed'.

Further up, on the left, is Boswell's Court, built for Thomas Lowthian *c.*1600 but named after a later owner, the doctor uncle of Johnson's biographer. James Boswell took Dr Johnson to see his uncle's museum there in 1773. Further up is Cannonball House, a late sixteenth-century structure so called because of the cannonball embedded in the fabric, allegedly fired by General Preston's artillery during the '45 but more mundanely said simply to mark the gravitation height reached by water from Comiston Springs. On the other side of the street is the Outlook Tower, whose four lower floors survive from an early seventeenth-century tenement. The building was reconstructed in 1853 to house Short's Observatory, when the top floor was replaced by two new floors with a battlemented parapet and an octagonal domed caphouse. Sir Patrick Geddes bought the building in 1892 and fitted it up as 'the world's first sociological laboratory', none of which survives. The Camera Obscura, still a tourist attraction, is housed in the battlemented ogee-capped tower.

2 (a) Castle Hill (1860s)

2 (b) Castle Hill (1987)

3   Lawnmarket, High Street: Head of West Bow

3 (a) W.D. Clark (*c.*1860), Scottish Photography Archive, Riddell Collection

3 (b) Murray Johnston (1987)

The upper stretch of the High Street, or Lawnmarket – a corruption of Landmarket, the place where the landward or country people set up their stalls on market days – has to the left Milne's Court, put up in 1690 by Robert Mylne; it is shown more clearly in Clark's photograph than in the modern one. Next to it is Gladstone's Land, now owned by the National Trust for Scotland, part of it rebuilt *c.*1740 and restored by Frank C. Mears in 1934–6. It was bought in 1617 by Thomas Gladstone, an ancestor of Prime Minister William Ewart Gladstone. Robert Hurd & Partners further restored the house in 1979–80, uncovering the fruit-and-flower-painted beam ceilings.

Further down from Gladstone's Land is the house in which Robert Burns lodged during the winter of 1786–7. Though the building itself was rebuilt following a fire in Victorian times, the tenements beyond the Burns house are all eighteenth century.

The most striking change is, of course, the disappearance of Bowhead House, the elaborately timbered building allegedly unsafe in the late 1870s but on which dynamite had to be used to bring about its demolition. In its place are tenements built in the 1880s, the corner tenement with crowstep gables and a three-storey oriel.

3 (b)

4 (a)

4   Lawnmarket

4 (a) Thomas Keith (*c*.1855), Edinburgh City Libraries

4 (b) Murray Johnston (1987)

In Keith's photograph, Gladstone's Land is on the extreme left. The small house with forestairs is Burns's lodging, replaced in the 1890s by a neo-seventeenth-century building. Beyond in the modern photograph is George S. Aitken's more extensive re-interpretation of a seventeenth-century Scots architectural style, carried out in 1897. The other two old buildings survive, that on the corner, once housing the business of Greig the printer, now being the Deacon Brodie Tavern.

5   City Chambers, High Street

5 (a) W.D. Clark (1860s), Scottish Photography Archive, Riddell Collection

5 (b) Murray Johnston (1987)

Built between 1753 and 1761, on the site of Sir Simon Preston's house (in which Mary, Queen of Scots, lodged the night before the Battle of Carberry Hill) under the act of 1753, secured by Lord Provost Drummond to allow 'the erecting [of] several publick buildings in the City of Edinburgh', the architect was John Adam. He designed a three-sided courtyard which opened onto the High Street. On the arcaded ground floor there were to be shops in the east and west ranges. The south side was closed, however, with a single-storey range of shops, giving rise to the effusion of a local rhymester with better architectural taste than poetic skill:

> The Royal Exchange, a building fine,
> Spoilt by some Council's love o' coin;
> The piazzas, once meant to be open,
> Are now completely filled wi' shoppin'.

When the Royal Exchange was first completed, the City Chambers occupied only a small section of it, but by 1762 the Council had taken over the entire block. By 1811, they had taken in the north block, and between 1849 and 1893 they occupied the rest of the building by stages. The south screen was rebuilt as an open arcade in 1900–1901. In 1930–4, E.J. MacRae extended the High Street frontage with matching wings.

5 (b)

6 Johnstone Terrace

6 (a) W.D. Clark (1860s), Scottish Photography Archive, Riddell Collection

6 (b) Murray Johnston (1987)

Clark's photograph shows dimly the spire of the former Tollbooth St John's Church. The old buildings in the foreground disappeared in Victorian times. In the modern photograph there can be seen the back of the church and the rear of Castlehill School, built by Robert Wilson in 1896 in a heavy baronial style, and a gabled tenement by Smith and Hardy, put up in 1864. This style of imitation pseudo-medieval 'land', or tenement, was popular with Victorian architects and is to be found in many parts of Edinburgh.

6 (a)

6 (b)

7 (a)

7 The Grassmarket

7 (a) W.D. Clark (*c*.1860), Scottish Photography Archive, Riddell Collection

7 (b) Murray Johnston (1987)

Clark's angle proved impossible to match today, possibly because he took his photograph standing on a cart. The Victorianization of the Grassmarket is obvious, to say nothing of the further loss of character it has sustained in our own time. It is now the site of several missions and hostels. Clark's photograph is a reminder that the Grassmarket was in times past the starting-place for carriers. At number 32, the White Horse Inn, a plaque commemorates Robert Burns's stay during his last visit to Edinburgh in 1791.

7 (b)

8 and 9   Greyfriars Churchyard and the Castle

8 (a) D.O. Hill/Robert Adamson (*c.*1845), Scottish Photography Archive

8 (b) and 8 (c) Murray Johnston (1987)

9 (a) D.O. Hill/Robert Adamson (*c.* 1845), Scottish Photography Archive

9 (b) Murray Johnston (1987)

Greyfriars Churchyard was founded in 1562, after Queen Mary had granted the garden of the Greyfriars Monastery to the town as a burial place to relieve the overcrowded churchyard of St Giles. In 1602 a church was built in the cemetery, though it was not opened until 1620. There are many fine seventeenth-century monuments in the churchyard, permission to erect such memorials being conditional on the payment of a considerable sum to the town council. By the early nineteenth century, Greyfriars Churchyard had become to John Wilson ('Christopher North', the friend of Sir Walter Scott and James Hogg) a 'huge auld red gloomy church' with 'a countless multitude o' grass graves a' touchin' ane anither'. Among the famous Scots buried there are Alexander Henderson, who in 1638 preached a sermon with a Covenant openly displayed in the church; the Regent Morton; George Buchanan, the Latin poet and tutor of Mary, Queen of Scots (who nevertheless gave evidence against her before her trial); Captain Porteus, the accidental instigator of the riots which bear his name and feature in Scott's novel *The Heart of Midlothian*; the statesman Duncan Forbes of Culloden and the poets Allan Ramsay and Duncan Ban MacIntyre.

Trees and shrubs have now obscured the modern view to the castle (8b). The modern shot from a slightly different angle (8c) reveals a twentieth-century intrusion that would be much better obscured.

Greyfriars was a favourite location for Hill and Adamson. The Naismith, Bethune and Denniston memorial stones are three of many with both monumental (9a and b) and historical interest.

8 (a)

8 (b)

8 (c) Greyfriars Churchyard and the Castle (1987)

9 (a) Greyfriars Churchyard (1987)

9 (b)   Greyfriars Churchyard (*c.*1845)

10 (a)

10   The Cowgate

10 (a) Attributed to W.D. Clark (*c.*1860), Scottish Photography Archive, Riddell Collection

10 (b) Murray Johnston (1987)

The Cowgate, now a dingy back street, once housed many of the famous, including the poet Bishop Gavin Douglas of Dunkeld. The elliptical St Cecilia's Hall of 1762, whose entrance is in the near off-right of Clark's photograph, was the last Edinburgh work of Robert Mylne, who is said to have based his design on Parma Opera House. It was to be the centre of Edinburgh music-making for the next fifty years. The Cowgate is nowadays further depressed by the heavy arches of the South Bridge and the George IV Bridge, depicted here, above which stands the extension to the National Library of Scotland. The bridge was built by Thomas Hamilton between 1834 and 1839 to mark the southern approach to the city, under the Improvement Act of 1827.

11 Advocates Close, High Street

11 (a) Archibald Burns (1860s), Scottish Photography Archive, Riddell Collection

11 (b) Murray Johnston (1987)

It is perhaps hard to believe that these two photographs depict the same close, running south, off the High Street. The older photograph was taken from further up the close, a viewpoint no longer available because of demolition.

Advocates Close, 357 High Street, once contained the residences of the legal luminaries Lord Westhall, Lord Advocate Stewart and Andrew Crosby, who became the prototype of Councillor Pleydell in Scott's *Guy Mannering*.

11 (a)

12 (a)

12 (b)

12 Moubray House and John Knox's House

12 (a) Archibald Burns (*c.*1870) Scottish Photography Archive, Riddell Collection

12 (b) Murray Johnston (1987)

The house with the forestairs, above the Edinburgh Woollen Mill shop, was probably built in 1529 by Andrew Moubray, a wright. It has similarities to Gladstone's Land, in the Lawnmarket. Next to Moubray House is the John Knox House, genuinely of the sixteenth century but unlikely to have had any connection with the Reformer. The fictitious association, however, has undoubtedly saved it from destruction on several occasions. It was restored by James Smith in 1850, and in 1981 the slate roof was replaced by a pantiled one. Incidentally, the Edinburgh Woollen Mill shop was for many years the premises of a celebrated antique-dealer.

13 (a)

13   Canongate Tollbooth

13 (a) Thomas Keith (*c.*1855), Royal Scottish Academy

13 (b) Murray Johnston (1987)

Keith favoured a high angle to feature Edinburgh's ancient seat of civic government and the town gaol, Canongate Tollbooth, dating from 1592. It is now a museum. The clock is early Victorian. The church, not shown in the picture, is by James Smith, opened in 1691. The railings of the churchyard can be seen in the modern photograph. It has many famous memorials, including that to Robert Fergusson, Edinburgh's Laureate, who died in 1774, the headstone being put up by Robert Burns in 1789. Burns's 'Clarinda', Mrs Agnes Maclehose, for whom he wrote 'Ae Fond Kiss', is buried nearby, as are her severe legal guardian, Lord Craig, and Burns's friend Professor Dugald Stewart.

13 (b)

14   *White Horse Close*

14 (a) Thomas Keith (*c.*1855), Royal Scottish Academy

14 (b) Murray Johnston (1987)

Laurence Ord built White Horse Close around a court in the late seventeenth century, the inn being the building at the north end. The whole composition was bought in 1889 and remodelled by James Jerdan as housing for the working classes. It was remodelled again by Frank Mears & Partners in 1962. Though, clearly, the remodelling has been extensive, the effect is not unpleasing. As one severe present-day critic put it, it is 'so blatantly fake that it can be acquitted of any intention to deceive' (*The Buildings of Edinburgh* by Gifford, McWilliam, Walker and Wilson).

There was another White Horse Inn – at the head of Canongate, in St Mary's Wynd, long since gone as a result of the Improvement Act of 1867 – where Johnson and Boswell stayed in 1773. But it was at the former coaching inn, featured here, that the fictional meeting between Edward Waverley and Fergus MacIvor in Scott's novel *Waverley* took place.

14 (a)

14 (b)

15 (a)

15 Queen Mary's Bathhouse

15 (a) W.D. Clark (late 1850s), Scottish Photography Archive, Riddell Collection

15 (b) Murray Johnston (1987)

This odd little building was originally a garden pavilion. It was left isolated when the surrounding wall was demolished in 1856–7 to allow the construction of the present approach to Holyrood. Its once handsome forestair was demolished in 1755. The old housing in Clark's photograph was cleared away under the Improvement Act of 1867, as in post-Second World War days were the tenements that replaced them.

15 (b)

16 and 17   Holyroodhouse

16 (a) Archibald Burns (*c.*1870), Scottish Photography Archive, Riddell Collection

16 (b) Murray Johnston (1987)

17 (a) Archibald Burns (1869), Scottish Photography Archive, Riddell Collection

17 (b) Murray Johnston (1987)

The Palace of Holyroodhouse dates from the early sixteenth century, though its present appearance is largely the work of Sir William Bruce. It was regularly used by James IV, James V, Mary, Queen of Scots, and James VI. The two Charleses only briefly used it, as did James, Duke of York, the future James II and VII, when he was Commissioner from 1679 to 1687. During the '45 Prince Charles Edward Stuart occupied it for six weeks, holding uneasy levees, since the castle at the top of the Royal Mile remained in government hands. Holyrood was then neglected – George IV entertained in it in 1822 but never stayed there – till Queen Victoria had it refurbished and returned it to royal residential use.

The large ornamental wrought-iron screens and gates (16b), replacing the more discreet older ones (16a), erected in 1912 in memory of Edward VII, were designed by Sir George Washington Browne and were modelled on Tijou's gates at Hampton Court. A lion and a unicorn adorn the piers.

Burns's photograph, looking towards Salisbury Crags (17a), shows the ruined abbey. Legend avers that David I, breaking a leg while out hunting on a forbidden holy day, was miraculously saved from death on the antlers of a stag, so built the abbey on the place of his deliverance by way of penance and thanksgiving. Nothing remains of his structure. The present nave is thought to date from between 1195 and 1230.

The abbey suffered during the invasion of the English Earl of Hertford in 1544 and was further damaged at the hands of the fanatical Protestant Earl of Glencairn in 1567, following the imprisonment of Queen Mary. Choir and transepts were demolished in 1570. The building had ceased to be the church for the Canongate parishioners in 1687. The Chapel Royal fittings were destroyed the following year, and the building entered a long period of neglect. In 1758 a stone slab roof placed over the high vault. Ten years later this led to the collapse of the vault, the clerestory and part of the north side. Restoration schemes were considered in 1906 and again in 1945 but on both occasions rejected on the grounds that too much new stonework would have to be added; which, on balance, perhaps seems a pity. Queen Victoria had the view of Holyrood from above engraved for publication in her book *Leaves from the Journal of Our Life in the Highlands*.

16 (a)

17 (a)   Holyroodhouse (1869)

17 (b)   Holyroodhouse (1987)

18   View from St Anthony's Chapel

18 (a) George Washington Wilson (undated), Scottish Photography Archive

18 (b) Murray Johnston (1987) *Photograph overleaf*

The chimneys have now gone, but the essential features of the scene remain: the rear corner of Holyrood, the Nelson and the National Monuments on Calton Hill, and the Georgian Royal and Regent Terraces beneath.

The clock tower of the North British Hotel, built between 1895 and 1902 to designs mainly by W. Hamilton Beattie, replaced a range of buildings by Richard Crichton, not clearly discernible in the older photograph.

18 (a)

19 (a)

19   St Margaret's Loch

19 (a) John Patrick (undated), Scottish Photography Archive, Riddell Collection

19 (b) Murray Johnston (1987)

The remains of St Anthony's Chapel, a late-medieval vaulted structure, stand perched on a crag above St Margaret's Loch in Holyrood Park. It is said to have been built by Abbot Bellenden, who founded a hospital for the poor and was responsible for the Holyrood *Ordinale*, a handsome parchment folio now shown in the palace gallery. Patrick's photograph, possibly dating from the 1880s, catches a lively exuberance, still occasionally matched by skaters today.

19 (b)

20 Duddingston Loch

20 (a) John Patrick (undated), Scottish Photography Archive, Riddell Collection

20 (b) Murray Johnston (1987)

Duddingston village and Loch lie south of Edinburgh, to the back of Arthur's Seat and Whinny Hill. The loch is strongly associated with skating because of the famous Raeburn painting of the Revd Robert Walker skating. The painter the Revd John Thomson, who died in 1840 and was buried in the churchyard, was an incumbent of the church. It is said that he was quite capable of cutting short a sermon if he thought a change in the weather would facilitate the work on his easel. The seventeenth-century church, which has eighteenth-century Gothic windows, originated in the twelfth century, being originally erected on land given by William the Lion to the monks of Kelso.

20 (a)

21 (a)

21 (b)

21   The Royal High School

21 (a) Archibald Burns (1869) Scottish Photography Archive, Riddell Collection

21 (b) Murray Johnston (1987)

It is sometimes claimed that the Royal High School has its antecedents in the twelfth century, a church school at Holyrood which in 1519 became a grammar school. By 1578 it had its own premises on the site of Blackfriars Cemetery, at the foot of Infirmary Street. A replacement building on the same site was put up in 1777.

Be that as it may, in 1822 a committee of Edinburgh subscribers, who included Sir Walter Scott and Lord Cockburn, proposed the building of a new independent school at Canonmills but were eventually persuaded that such a school should be built in the city, in association with the old Royal High School. The first plan was by William Burn, but it greatly exceeded the budget, so the Greek Doric temple which eventually went up between 1825 and 1829 is by Thomas Hamilton. In the 1960s the school moved to a modern suburban building, and between 1977 and 1980 the original school was adapted for the use of the Scottish Assembly which, failing to clear the heavily slanted referendum hurdle of 1978, has yet to come into being. Before the building's conversion, it was occasionally used by the Edinburgh International Festival, the most distinguished production staged in it being Allan Ramsay's pastoral opera *The Gentle Shepherd*.

22   Calton Hill and the National Monument

22 (a) Archibald Burns (1860s), National Monuments Record

22 (b) Murray Johnston (1987)

Sir William Playfair was the architect of the grandiose unfinished memorial to the Scots killed in the Napoleonic Wars, a copy of the western range of the Parthenon. The work, which was to cost £50,000, was begun in 1824, the foundation stone having been laid by George IV two years before. Each of its fluted columns cost £1,000. After ten columns had been erected, the money ran out and the building was never completed, perhaps fortunately. As a ruin, its tracery dignifies the Edinburgh skyscape. The building, had it been finished, would have been a church. Scott and Cockburn were again amongst the promoters, as was Lord Elgin, of Elgin Marbles fame.

To the left stands the Nelson Monument, south-east of the Observatory. It was designed in 1807 by Robert Burn. The top section supports cross-trees and a time ball, fitted in 1852, giving a visual signal at noon to ships in the Forth. It was once connected electrically with Edinburgh Castle, the ball dropping to coincide with the firing of the one o'clock gun. The rooms surrounding the base, once a restaurant, now form a private house.

22 (b)

23   The Dugald Stewart Monument

23 (a) Archibald Burns (1860s), National Monuments Record

23 (b) Murray Johnston (1987)

As well as being the architect of the National Monument, Playfair was also responsible for the Dugald Stewart Monument, copied from the Choragic Monument of Lysicrates. Stewart, Professor of Moral Philosophy at Edinburgh University from 1785 to 1810, was a much-valued friend of Robert Burns. He had a country estate at Catrine, in Ayrshire, where the poet was a frequent visitor.

23 (a)

23 (b)

24 Rock House, Calton Hill

24 (a) Archibald Burns (*c*.1870), Edinburgh City Libraries

24 (b) Murray Johnston (1987)

Though not even marked by a plaque, this unassuming villa, dating from the early nineteenth century, is one of the most important sites in relation to the history of photography, for in 1843 Robert Adamson rented it to use as his studio. The photographic association continued with D.O. Hill, Thomas Annan, who later set up his own studio in Glasgow, Archibald Burns and Francis Caird Inglis.

In 1851 it was bought by the Town Council, who proposed to demolish it and re-erect on the site Trinity College Church (photograph 25), which in its turn was taken down to make way for Waverley Station. The church, however, was rebuilt in Jeffrey Street, and Hill continued to rent Rock House. Today it is a private residence, now closely sheltered by mature trees.

24 (a)

24 (b)

25   Trinity College Church

25 (a) D.O. Hill/Robert Adamson (*c.*1845), Scottish Photography Archive

25 (b) and (c) Murray Johnston (1987)

Trinity College was founded by Mary of Gueldres, James II's queen, shortly before 1460, in the valley between the Old Town and Calton Hill. The building was never fully completed, although the choir and transepts served as a parish church from just after the Reformation until 1848, when the North British Railway bought the site. The church was carefully dismantled under the supervision of David Bryce, the stones being numbered for rebuilding on the present site, between the High Street and Jeffrey Street. Unfortunately, the rebuilding was not begun until 1872, and whilst lying on the Calton Hill many of the stones were stolen. As a result, only the choir, without aisles or transepts, was re-erected. In the modern photograph the numbering on some of the stones may still be seen.

25 (c)   Trinity College Church (1987)

26   Calton Hill and Waverley Station

26 (a) George Washington Wilson (1880s), Scottish Photography Archive, Riddell Collection

26 (b) Murray Johnston (1987)

Wilson's photograph shows the City Observatory, on the west summit of Calton Hill, a domed building put up by Playfair in 1818 as an astronomical institution. This had been founded in 1812, with Professor John Playfair, the architect's uncle, as President. The towered Gothic Observatory was begun by James Craig in 1776 but not completed until 1792, possibly with some design work by Adam. To the right, more clearly visible in the modern picture, is Playfair's own monument to his uncle, a square tetrastyle Greek Doric arrangement of columns on a podium. The obelisk monument, put up in 1845 by Thomas Hamilton, commemorates the Friends of the People martyrs, Muir, Palmer, Skirving, Gerrald and Margarot, tried in 1794 and deported, much to the indignation of Robert Burns.

To the right is the battlemented, towered and turreted Gaol Governor's House by Archibald Elliot, put up between 1815 and 1817, and all that remains of the old Calton Gaol. Adam was responsible for the Bridewell section in 1791, initiating the castellated motif. Archibald Elliot's section, the middle group, went up between 1884 and 1887 replacing the old Tollbooth in the High Street. The battlemented wall is also Elliot's.

The Adam and Elliot gaols were demolished to make way for Thomas S. Tait's St Andrews House, which was built between 1936 and 1939. It is now called Old St Andrews House, New St Andrews House being a depressing factory-like erection on the site of the old St James's Square. Tait's St Andrews House bears some relation to the League of Nations building at Geneva and is probably the most significant piece of public architecture to have gone up during the thirties. Together with New St Andrews House, it still houses the Scottish Office, the local seat of London government.

In both photographs Waverley Station fills the valley beneath. There were originally three railway termini operated by different companies, lying, as it were, end to end. The joint station for two of the lines may have been designed by David Bell. The third line, that of the Edinburgh, Perth & Dundee Railway, opened in 1847 and ran at right-angles to the others through the Scotland Street Tunnel, connecting Edinburgh, Leith and the Newhaven ferry terminus, opened in 1842. This became the main crossing-point over the Forth prior to the building of the Forth Bridge.

A replacement station, taking in the vegetable market to the south of the railway lines, was built between 1874 and 1876 by Robert Morham, at which time the roofing-in was completed.

26 (a)   Calton Hill and Waverley Station (1880s)

26 (b)   Calton Hill and Waverley Station (1987)

27   *Waverley Market and Princes Street*

27 (a) attributed to J.G. Tunny (1860s), Scottish Photography Archive, Riddell Collection *Photograph overleaf*

27 (b) Murray Johnston (1987)

Robert Morham (see 26) also built the Waverley Market, demolished in 1974 to be replaced a decade later with the prismatic concrete erection in the foreground of the modern photograph. Then, as now, the Scott Monument dominated the south side of Princes Street.

27 (b)

28 (a)

28   The Scott Monument

28 (a) W.H. Fox Talbot (1844), Scottish Photography Archive, Riddell Collection

28 (b) D.O. Hill/Robert Adamson (1845), Scottish Photography Archive, Riddell Collection

28 (c) D.O. Hill/Robert Adamson (1844), Scottish Photography Archive, Riddell Collection

28 (d) and (e) Murray Johnston (1987)

The Scott Monument in its uncompleted state is the only image common to the greatest exponents of calotype photography. It stands 200 feet high and was the work of George Meikle Kemp, a Border shepherd who became a carpenter and a self-taught architect. He worked for a time in the office of William Burn, travelling Europe to study Gothic architecture. After Scott's death in 1832 a competition was held to choose a design for a monument to him. Kemp's plans came third, but nevertheless he got the job. The structure was completed in 1846, two years after Kemp was found drowned in the Union Canal.

The central statue of Sir Walter, seated with his dog Maida, was sculpted out of Carrara marble by Sir John Steell. Many sculptors contributed statues of Scott's characters.

Melrose Abbey, Glasgow Cathedral and even the towers of Reims Cathedral, as well as details from the cathedral spire at Antwerp, apparently influenced Kemp. Though mocked by Ruskin as 'a small vulgar Gothic steeple on the ground', it remains an instantly recognizable tribute to the writer who, more than anyone else, made the story of the great historical confrontations of Scottish history available to the ordinary man through the Waverley Novels, arousing also the interest of Romantic Europe in Scotland. Along with Robert Burns, who saved the Scots tongue from extinction when it was in danger of being anglified out of existence (there is a Lysicratic monument to him on the Calton Hill), Scott helped to rescue the sense of national identity when Scotland the Nation was in danger of being pressurized into becoming a gentilified North Britain.

28 (b) The Scott Monument (1845)

28 (c)   The Scott Monument (1844)

28 (d)   The Scott Monument (1987)

28 (e)   The Scott Monument (1987)

29   The Castle from East Princes Street Gardens

29 (a) Archibald Burns (*c.*1870), Scottish Photography Archive, Riddell Collection

29 (b) Murray Johnston (1987)

East Princes Street Gardens were laid out in 1830 by Patrick Neill but rearranged between 1849 and 1850 by David Cousin in the manner shown in Burns's photograph. Today the layout is less formal, in accordance with modern taste.

29 (b)

29 (a)

30 (a)

30   Bank of Scotland

30 (a) W.D. Clark (*c*.1858), Scottish Photography Archive, Riddell Collection

30 (b) Murray Johnston (1987)

The Bank of Scotland received its charter in 1695, when it was originally located in Old Bank Close. This building was demolished when the street line of the George IV Bridge was established. The original building on the present site, shown on Clark's photograph, was designed by Robert Reid and Richard Crichton, and completed between 1802 and 1806. Its north elevation was much disliked. Several architects, including Thomas Hamilton, drew up alteration plans but finally, in 1863, David Bryce was brought in to remodel it. His work was completed between 1868 and 1870. If the original bank suggested an overgrown Georgian country house, the final result certainly resembles an ornate Italianate palace.

31   Royal Scottish Academy

31 (a) Archibald Burns (undated), National Monuments Record

31 (b) Murray Johnston (1987)

The Royal Scottish Academy, at the north end of the Mound, was built by Sir William Playfair in the pure Greek Doric style of the time of Pericles, between 1822 and 1826 and 1831 and 1836, for the Board of Manufactures and Fisheries, who accommodated the Royal Society, the Institution for the Encouragement of Fine Arts and the Society of Antiquaries. It is constructed of a mixture of Culallo and Craigleith stone. In 1844 the statue of Queen Victoria, dressed as Britannia, by Sir John Steell was perched, rather oddly, on the north pediment.

Behind it, and just perceptible in the modern photograph, is the National Gallery, also designed by Playfair. It went up between 1850 and 1854 and now houses the most comprehensive collection of Scottish paintings from the seventeenth to the nineteenth century, as well as the loaned masterpieces of Lord Ellesmere's Bridgewater Collection.

31 (a)

31 (b)

32 (a)

32   The National Gallery and Royal Institution

32 (a) W.D. Clark (*c*.1858), Scottish Photography Archive, Riddell Collection

32 (b) Murray Johnston (1987)

The Ionic columns of the National Gallery, looking towards the Royal Scottish Academy and Princes Street. As can be seen from this photograph, the two galleries are not as axially lined as would appear in photographs taken from Princes Street. The modern building in Princes Street is the New Club, which went up in 1966, the work of Alan Reiach. On this and the adjacent site formerly stood an 1834 building by William Burn and the magnificent Baroque Life Association Palace of 1855 by David Rhind. The destruction of the Rhind building led to much controversy and the threat by one of the authors of the invaluable Edinburgh volume in Pevsner's *The Buildings of Scotland* series to lie down in front of the bulldozers. He changed his mind.

32 (b)

33   Princes Street

33 (a) W.D. Clark (*c.*1858), Scottish Photography Archive, Riddell Collection

33 (b) Murray Johnston (1987)

Some idea of the quality of the lost Rhind building can be gained from this Clark photograph. It has a fine sense of atmosphere, although, of course, it does not capture the Calton Hill in the background, as does its modern counterpart, which shows the Nelson Monument in its piled-up 'bobbin-reel' aspect. The setts certainly made a much more sympathetic street flooring than their tarmacadam modern counterpart but were, of course, wholly impractical on a main traffic-bearing street.

33 (a)

33 (b)

34   Allan Ramsay Monument

34 (a) Archibald Burns (1860s), National Monuments Record

34 (b) Murray Johnston (1987)

Allan Ramsay, commemorated since 1865 by Sir John Steell's statue in West Princes Street Gardens, was an important figure in the history of Edinburgh and of Scottish literature. He played a pioneering part in founding the eighteenth-century Literary Revival of the Scots tongue, which culminated with Robert Burns. As an enthusiastic collector and, by his way of it, 'improver' ('gentilifier' would have have been a more accurate description) of Scots folk-song, a pioneering anthology of which he published under the title *The Tea Table Miscellany* between 1724 and 1732, and as the reviver of interest in the Scottish Makars (as the 'Scottish Chaucerians' are more properly called in Scotland) in his *Evergreen* anthology of 1724, he brought to the attention of his contemporaries, to say nothing of those who came after, the fundamental achievement of the national literary heritage. His own most important original contributions to Scottish poetry were his mock-elegies in Scots on such well-known local characters as the brothel-keeper Lucky Spence and Maggy Johnston, who ran a celebrated ale-house just outside Edinburgh. His pastoral opera of 1725, *The Gentle Shepherd*, whose songs were set to folk-airs, preceded John Gay's *The Beggar's Opera* by three years.

From his bookshop in the High Street he founded the city's first circulating library and, but for the machinations of the Kirk, would also have succeeded in establishing in Carruber's Close a regular theatre several decades before the anti-theatre prejudices of ministers of religion were finally put to flight by the Revd Alexander ('Jupiter') Carlyle.

Ramsay's statue now contains in its base the mechanism of Edinburgh's floral cuckoo clock, set into the bank to the left of the modern photograph, though the cuckoo's 'house' is shown. On the hill, in the background, are Ramsay Gardens, so called because the second house from west to east incorporates Ramsay Lodge, the unusual turreted and pinnacled house partly designed by the poet *c.*1740 with some assistance from his portrait-painting son, also Allan Ramsay. Alterations were made to Ramsay Lodge in 1856 by R.W. Billings.

34 (b)   Allan Ramsay Monument (1987)

35 George Street (East)

35 (a) W.D. Clark (*c*.1860), Scottish Photography Archive, Riddell Collection

35 (b) Murray Johnston (1987)

The land to the north of the Nor' Loch, drained in 1763, and the valley where Waverley Station now lies, was without houses (except for the mansion of Easter Coates, built in 1600 and, with later additions, now the deanery to St Mary's Episcopalian Cathedral) until Lord Provost Drummond promoted a competitive scheme for the development of the New Town, as it was to be called. The competition was won by James Craig in 1768. It envisaged Princes Street, one-sided and facing the castle; George Street, on the crest of the spine; and Queen Street, on the northern slopes which eventually lead down to the Firth of Forth. The streets were to be laterally linked and meaner service streets were to be built between them. This plan was adhered to for about thirty years and supplemented by several further plans carried out in the Georgian spirit until the late 1840s, when Victorianism took over. The result is the finest piece of co-ordinated planned Georgian township in Europe, an excellence of design and execution which neither late Victorian and Edwardian neglect, mid-twentieth century developers' greed nor planners' insensitivity did much significantly to erode.

George Street, named after George IV, whose visit to Edinburgh in 1822 was stage-managed largely by Sir Walter Scott (as a result of which the portly monarch appeared in a kilt), was originally conceived as the main street of Craig's plan. The general run of the domestic architecture was simple, the grandeur being reserved for Robert Adam's Charlotte Square, at the west end of the street, and St Andrew Square at the east end. Adam did not live to complete Charlotte Square, and in the event St Andrew Square was left for others to execute.

The centrepiece of St Andrew Square, now the head office of the Royal Bank of Scotland, was designed by William Chambers in 1771 as a New Town mansion for Sir Laurence Dundas. It may be seen, dwarfed by Edinburgh's bus station, in the modern photograph.

The tall Doric column in the middle of the square, modelled by William Burn on that of Trajan in Rome, commemorates Henry Dundas, first Viscount Melville, and was raised between 1821 and 1828. The statue is by Robert Forrest. The first building on the left, best seen in the modern photograph, is a neo-Palladian structure which went up between 1897 and 1901, the pediment, to be seen in the older photograph, having been taken from an 1839 building on the site by David Bryce. Next in the modern picture there is the Renaissance-style 1898 Royal Insurance Company building by Hamilton Beatty.

Then comes St Andrew's Church, prominently featured in both photographs, oval in plan and the first to be built in the New Town. It was designed by Major Andrew Fraser, a Royal Engineer (who became Scottish Engineer-in-Chief in 1779) and was put up between 1782 and 1787, Alexander Sibbald's elegant steeple being added later.

Patronage in the filling of ministerial vacancies was re-introduced to Scottish Church government after the Union of 1707. The more evangelical ministers, who had gradually increased in number over the previous fifty years, found more difficulty in getting 'livings' from the landowning patrons. The crisis came in 1843 when, following a gathering in St Andrew's Church, 470 ministers, elders and members, led by Dr Thomas Chalmers, walked out not only from St Andrew's but from the Church of Scotland itself, to found the Free Church, thus creating a schism that was not to be healed until 1929, by which time the coming-together was of far less general social significance than the original split had been. It was in order to make calotypes as preliminary sketches, to record the Disruption in a painting, that Hill and Adamson were brought together.

Next to the church is the George Hotel, which evolved out of three houses dating from the 1780s. The Corinthian portico was added over one of them by David Bryce in 1840, and by McGibbon & Ross over the others in 1879. Chantry's statue of George IV was put up in 1831 to commemorate his 1822 visit.

35 (a)   George Street (East) (*c.*1860)

35 (b)   George Street (East) (1987)

36 George Street (West)

36 (a) George Washington Wilson (1870s), Scottish Photography Archive, Riddell Collection

36 (b) Murray Johnston (1987)

Silhouetted in the foreground by both photographers is the statue of William Pitt by Francis Chantrey. The north side of Washington Wilson's photograph shows many of the original buildings, replaced in the modern photograph by something of a mish-mash.

The front of St George's Church, designed to be the western climax of the first New Town, was begun in 1811, not to Adam's original design but to an altered design by Robert Reid. It was opened in 1814 and went out of use as a place of worship after the Second World War. During the 1960s it was altered to fulfil its present purpose as West Register House.

37 (a)

37 (b)

37   Moray Place

37 (a) Dr William Robertson (*c.*1855), Private collection

37 (b) Murray Johnston (1987)

The tenth Earl of Moray inherited a site of some thirty acres which had been acquired by his father in 1782 from the Heriot Trust, to enlarge his existing house. In 1822 the eleventh Earl decided that it should be feued for development and engaged James Gillespie Graham to draw up plans. The construction of these included Ainslie Place, Albion Place, Darnaway Street, Randolph Crescent and, grandest of all, Moray Place. Several of the houses have magnificent interiors, number 27 in particular. In some cases twentieth-century subdivision into flats has lessened the impact. Number 28, the Earl of Moray's own house, though flatted, still preserves remarkably fine interiors.

38   Queensferry Street

38 (a) A.C. Inglis (undated), Edinburgh City Libraries

38 (b) Murray Johnston (1987)

To the right in both photographs is the corner of Randolph Crescent. The L-plan house in the foreground, to the left of the bridge, under scaffolding in the modern photograph, is Kirkbrae House. It was originally a seventeenth- or eighteenth-century tavern for the village baxters, or bakers. It carries a seventeenth-century stone of a judge's head taken from demolished Dean House, and a cartouche from one of the baxters' houses in Dean Village. In 1892 it became part of a Scottish Baronial style remodelling and extension by J. Graham Finlay. While from the photographer's angle it looks as if it rises to only two storeys, from Miller Row, at the front of the cliff to the back, it is seen to have five storeys and to be turreted.

38 (a)

38 (b)

39 The Dean Bridge

39 (a) Archibald Burns (1860s), Edinburgh City Libraries

39 (b) Murray Johnston (1987)

Built by Thomas Telford in 1831–2 to link Lord Moray's estate with the Learmonth Estate, on the south of the Water of Leith (Edinburgh's domestic river), the Dean Bridge was designed to provide an imposing approach to the New Town houses from the far bank. It is a four-arched structure rising to over a hundred feet above the Water of Leith. The parapets were heightened in 1912 to discourage suicides. Underneath, a footpath runs along the south bank. Mature trees somewhat obscure the modern view of the bridge.

40 (a)

40   St Bernard's Well

40 (a) W.D. Clark (1858), Scottish Photography Archive, Riddell Collection

40 (b) Murray Johnston (1987)

The circular Roman temple, on the south bank of the Water of Leith, was commissioned from Alexander Nasmyth, the painter, in 1788, by Lord Gardenstone, a wealthy landlord who believed his health had benefited from the mineral spring. It replaced an earlier wellhouse of 1760. Under the layered dome is the statue of Hygeia, replacing the original of 1791. The present sculpture, by D.W. Stevenson, was positioned in 1888, when the pump room was refitted by Thomas Bonnar. The growth of the woodlands made it impossible for a modern shot to be taken at the exact position of the original. Murray Johnston therefore took his photograph from a position a little downstream.

40 (b)

41 (a)

41   Colinton Manse

41 (a) D.O. Hill/Robert Adamson (1844), Scottish Photography Archive

41 (b) Murray Johnston (1987)

Colinton Manse, old and thickly wooded even in the boyhood days of R.L. Stevenson, who thought it 'a place like no other', is now almost totally obscured by trees. Stevenson's grandfather was once the incumbent. The early nineteenth-century building has been altered little externally since Stevenson's time.

41 (b)

42 and 43   *Craigmillar Castle*

42 (a) Scottish Photography Archive, Riddell Collection

42 (b) Murray Johnston (1987)

43 (a) W.D. Clark (*c.*1858), Scottish Photography Archive, Riddell Collection

43 (b) Murray Johnston (1987)

The Preston family acquired Craigmillar Castle in the late fourteenth century, incidentally also presenting St Giles's armbone to what was then Edinburgh parish church. At one time James III imprisoned his own brother, the Earl of Mar, in it. Looted by Hertford's invading army, to whom in 1544 it was forced to surrender, it was repaired. In 1566 Mary, Queen of Scots, spent an unhappy week in it, for at Craigmillar Moray, Lethington and Bothwell held the secret 'Conference of Craigmillar', urging her to divorce Darnley. The core of the castle was the tower house, seen in both photographs. The modern photographs (42b and 43b) illustrate particularly the once-imposing Banqueting Hall, 36 feet long and 22 feet wide.

42 (a)

42 (b)

43 (a) Craigmillar Castle (*c.*1858)

43 (b) Craigmillar Castle (1987)

44   Forth Railway Bridge

44 (a) John Patrick (undated), Scottish Photography Archive, Riddell Collection *Photograph overleaf*

44 (b) Murray Johnston (1987)

The Forth Railway Bridge, one of the wonders of Victorian engineering, is a steel cantilever structure with central connecting girders. It was designed by Sir John Fowler, Benjamin Baker and William Arrol, the two latter being knighted for their achievement when the bridge was opened by the Prince of Wales (later King Edward VII) on 4 March 1890. The original designs by Sir Thomas Bouch envisaged a suspension bridge, but after the disastrous collapse of the Tay Bridge in 1879 both the idea of a suspension bridge and Bouch's designs were abandoned. As can be seen in the older photograph, one cantilever rests on the island of Inchgarvie.

Almost underneath the Forth Bridge, on the other side of the river, is the Hawes Inn, built in 1683. Stevenson is said to have begun writing *Kidnapped* in Room 13, and here his Captain Hoseason and Ebenezer Balfour plotted the kidnapping of young David. Scott also used it for a scene in his novel *The Antiquary*. To the far side of the bridge the jetty used by the car-ferry survives. This Queensferry crossing goes back to medieval times but was finally superseded in 1964, when the Forth Road Bridge, upstream from the railway bridge, was opened.

44 (b)

45   The Panorama

45 (a), (c), (e) and (g) D.O. Hill/Robert Adamson (*c*.1845), Glasgow University Library

45 (b), (d), (f) and (h) Murray Johnston (1987)

About 1846 D.O. Hill produced a painting which he called 'Edinburgh – Old and New'. Now in the National Gallery of Scotland, it shows the city from a viewpoint high in the castle. Much of it coincides with the images in the series of four calotypes reproduced here. There is no doubt that Hill used the photographs as sketches for the painting, just as he did for the Disruption painting in making the portraits of the Free Kirk ministers. Indeed, one of the prints of the 'panorama' calotypes has traces of paint on it.

In the modern photograph, in which the scope of the older panorama is matched with great skill by Murray Johnston, the castle esplanade is shown with the stand for the Tattoo, an auxiliary of the Edinburgh International Festival of Music and Drama, whose construction and taking-down occupy approximately four months of every year. The smoke-filled atmosphere of the earlier photograph explains the origin of Edinburgh's ancient nickname 'Auld Reekie'.

In Hill and Adamson's picture the Waverley Market had not yet been built, nor, of course, the North British Hotel. Only one railway line appears to lead into what was to become the Waverley terminus. It is also notable that the National Gallery had not yet been constructed.

45 (a)   *c.*1845

45 (b)   1987

45 (c) *c.*1845
45 (d) 1987

45 (e) *c.*1845
45 (f) 1987

45 (g) *c.*1845
45 (h) 1987

Bibliography

New Edinburgh, Auld Reekie

Boswell, James, *The Life of Samuel Johnson* (London, 1791)

Cockburn, Henry, *Memorials of His Time* (Edinburgh, 1852)

Dunbar, William, *The Poems of William Dunbar* (ed. W. Mackay Mackenzie, London, 1932)

Fergusson, Robert, *The Poems of Robert Fergusson* (Scottish Text Society, 1956)

Fraser, G.S., *Collected Poems* (Leicester, 1981)

Garioch, R., *Collected Poems* (Loanhead, 1977)

Gifford, John, McWilliam, Colin, Walker, David, and Wilson, C., *Edinburgh* (Harmondsworth, 1984)

Lindsay, M., *Robert Burns: the Man; his Life; the Legend* (4th ed., London, 1989)

Lindsay, M., *Count All Men Mortal: The Story of Scottish Provident* (Edinburgh, 1987)

Lindsay, M., *The Discovery of Scotland* (London, 1969)

Lindsay, M., *The Eye is Delighted: Some Romantic Travellers in Scotland* (London, 1970)

Lockhart, J., *Peter's Letters to his Kinsfolk* (London, 1817)

MacCaig, N., *Collected Poems* (London, 1988)

MacLaren, M., *The Capital of Scotland* (Edinburgh, 1975)

Smith, S.G., *Collected Poems* (London, 1950)

Stevenson, R.L., *Edinburgh: Picturesque Notes* (Edinburgh, 1879)

Todd, R., *Garland for a Winter Solstice* (London, 1981)

Youngson, A.J., *The Making of Classical Edinburgh* (Edinburgh, 1966)

Edinburgh and the Photographers

Annan, Thomas, *Photographs of the Old Closes and Streets of Glasgow 1868/1877* (Dover, New York, 1977)

Bruce, David, *Sun Pictures – The Hill Adamson Calotypes* (Studio Vista, 1973)

Coburn, Alvin Langdon, (ed. Gernsheim) *Autobiography* (Faber, 1966)

Gernsheim, Helmut, *Lewis Carroll* (Dover, New York, 1969)

Gernsheim, Helmut, *The Origins of Photography* (Thames & Hudson, 1982)

Gernsheim, Helmut and Alison, *L.J.M. Daguerre* (Dover, New York, 1968)

(Ed.) Green, Jonathon, *Camera Work – a Critical Anthology* (Aperture Press, New York, 1973)

Hannavy, John, *Thomas Keith's Scotland* (Cannongate, Edinburgh, 1981)

Hyde, Ralph, *Panoramania!* (Trefoil Publications, 1988)

Lassam, Robert, *Fox Talbot, Photographer* (Compton Press, 1979)

(Ed.) Morrison-Low, A.D. and Christie, J.R.R., *Martyr of Science – Sir David Brewster* (Royal Scottish Museum, Edinburgh, 1984)

Stevenson, Robert Louis, *Edinburgh* (with 23 photographs by Alvin Langdon Coburn) (Rupert Hart-Davis, 1954)

Stevenson, Sara, *David Octavius Hill and Robert Adamson – Calotypes* (catalogue) (HMSO, Edinburgh, 1981)

Taylor, Roger, *George Washington Wilson* (Aberdeen University Press, 1981)

Ward, John and Stevenson, Sara, *Printed Light* (HMSO, Edinburgh, 1986)

Index

References in **bold** indicate illustrations.